Unstoppable Belief

11 Keys To Help You Be Persistent,
Keep On Going,
And Never Give Up On Your Goals And
Dreams!

WARNING: IMPLEMENT WHEN YOU'RE READY
FOR IMMEDIATE CLARITY, FOCUS, AND
SUCCESS.

Self-Published by Cristian Martinez

DEDICATION

Unstoppable Belief is dedicated to my amazing children, Deonte, Jaylen, and Genesis. I encourage each of you to dream big, no matter what life shows you. You have incredible potential and gifts beyond what you can see right now. My hope is that you will make the impact you were created for, never giving up on your dreams and goals.

To my wife, Sharita, a phenomenal woman of faith, a powerful prayer warrior, and my greatest support, this journey has been extraordinary because of your unwavering love and encouragement. Thank you for walking beside me with strength, grace, and belief through every season.

Unstoppable Belief

My Gift To You: Bonus Resource for Investing In Yourself. Please go to the page below, enter your email address, and get access to the Unstoppable Belief Companion workbook.

https://www.unstoppablebelief.com/free-resources

Table of Contents

1. Dedication
2. Introduction: The Journey of Unstoppable Belief Mindset
3. Chapter 0: Your Unique Design
   - Overview of the book's.
   - How can this book support you in achieving your goals?

Part I: Foundations for Success
4. Chapter 1: Complete Optimization
   - Focusing on health, environment, energy management, and goal visibility.
5. Chapter 2: Leaving Your Comfort Zone
   - Embracing growth through small risks and the power of stepping beyond familiarity.
6. Chapter 3: Embracing Mistakes
   - Learning from setbacks, celebrating small failures, and reframing mistakes as opportunities.

Part II: Attention to Your Strength
7. Chapter 4: Mastering Self-talk
   - Building a positive inner dialogue through affirmations, self-compassion, and visualization.
8. Chapter 5: Your Most Valuable Asset
   - Identifying and investing in personal strengths, passions, and growth.
9. Chapter 6: The Power Shift
   - Moving from a reactive mindset to a proactive approach, taking control of your life.

Part III: Strengthening Your Resolve
10. Chapter 7: Building Resilience
   - Using self-reflection to reinforce resilience and learn from experiences.

11. Chapter 8: Practicing Patience
   o Embracing long-term goals, celebrating small wins, and staying connected to purpose.

Part IV: Tools for Achieving Your Dreams

11. Chapter 9: Mastering Focus
   o Cultivating deep work, eliminating distractions, and setting clear priorities.
12. Chapter 10: Create Accountability
   o Building a support system, setting public commitments, and celebrating milestones with accountability partners.
13. Chapter 11: Overcoming Self-Sabotage
   o Recognizing self-sabotaging behaviors, challenging limiting beliefs, and replacing them with empowering habits.

Stay The Course Closing Reflections

14. Chapter 12: Embracing an Unstoppable Belief Mindset
   o Staying committed to growth, celebrating the small wins, staying anchored, and don't do it alone, living with unstoppable belief, and final thoughts
15. Unstoppable Belief Framework
16. About the Author

INTRODUCTION

The Journey of Unstoppable Belief. What is Unstoppable Belief? Unstoppable belief is the courage to move forward when you don't fully believe in yourself yet, so you lean on the faith, encouragement, or support of someone who does.

It's what keeps you going while your own confidence is still catching up. And over time, that Unstoppable belief becomes your own.

Life is a journey filled with peaks of triumph and valleys of challenge. It's in those valleys when you feel like giving up that your resilience is tested and strengthened. This book is a guide. A companion to help you navigate those moments and emerge stronger, more determined, and fully capable of achieving your goals.

At its heart, Unstoppable Belief is about discovering and embracing the power already inside you. It's about shifting the story from "never give up" to "never give up on you" on your dreams, your goals, and your unique potential.

This isn't just a story of perseverance. It's a journey of building the habits, mindsets, and systems that help you move forward even when the road feels uncertain. Whether you're facing professional challenges, personal setbacks, or moments of self-doubt, this book is a reminder: Resilience isn't reserved for the extraordinary; it's a skill anyone can develop.

Through practical steps, relatable stories, and time-tested principles, you'll discover tools to unlock your best self and align your life with your vision.

This book isn't just about inspiration, it's about transformation. Each chapter gives you insights and simple, powerful actions you can take right where you are.

By the final page, you'll have a roadmap for building unshakable resilience, overcoming obstacles, and achieving what matters most. We'll celebrate small wins, simplify the complex, and uncover the strength that's been within you all along. As you turn the page, come with an open heart, a willing mind, and a readiness to rise. This is your moment to dig deep, stay grounded, and show yourself what you're truly capable of. Let's begin this journey of Unstoppable belief not just in your dreams, but in you.

CHAPTER 0: YOUR UNIQUE DESIGN

How DISC Helps You Borrow My Belief in You

We all show up to life differently. Some of us are bold and direct. Others are thoughtful and reserved. Some draw energy from people, while others refuel in quiet moments. That's not a flaw, that's design.

In this book, I intentionally use the DISC personality model to help people from all walks of life apply the tools they need to overcome fear, develop resilience, and refuse to give up on themselves or their dreams.

What is DISC?

DISC is a simple yet powerful framework for understanding your personality style—and how you naturally respond to challenges, people, and goals. It's not about labeling. It's about unlocking.

Type	Meaning	Strengths	Growth Area
D	Dominant	Driven, Decisive, Results-Focused	May struggle with patience or empathy
I	Influential	Enthusiastic, People-Oriented	Needs help with follow-through
S	Steady	Loyal, Supportive, Consistent	Can resist change or risk
C	Conscientious	Detail-Oriented, Analytical	May overthink or fear mistakes

DISC isn't here to put you in a box—it's a mirror. It helps you understand your wiring so you can grow with grace.

Why I Use DISC in This Book

This book isn't one-size-fits-all, because you're not. Each of the 11 keys includes four practical pillars. These pillars aren't just habits—they're flexible tools that speak to the strengths and needs of each DISC type:

D types feel empowered by vision, clarity, and measurable goals.

I types thrive on creativity, encouragement, and relationships.

S types grow through consistency, support, and steady pacing.

C types lean into structure, reflection, and precision.

My goal is simple: help you see yourself in every chapter so you can find what fits, stretch where needed, and keep showing up. Each chapter in this book includes four practical steps designed to help you grow with clarity and purpose. You'll also notice that each step is intentionally aligned with an action that best fits a specific DISC personality type.

If you're curious about why each step connects to a particular style, feel free to flip to Chapter 13 in the back of the book for a quick reference and deeper insight.

For Every Background, Every Dreamer

Whether you're a professional, entrepreneur, student, military veteran, ministry leader, or someone navigating life transitions, this book is for you. DISC transcends personality and culture. It gives us language for self-awareness, grace for our weaknesses, and a strategy for helping our God-given dreams take shape. This is about personal empowerment for every personality, every background, and every dream.

A Note of Hope

God created you with a purpose. Your personality isn't a problem; it's part of that purpose. And when you understand it, you can walk with greater clarity and confidence.

Before we go further, I invite you to make this declaration:

"I give myself permission to grow my way, in my timing, with God's help."

The tools are here. The pillars are aligned. And through DISC, you'll learn not just how to borrow my belief in you, *never give up* on your dream, your goals, and how to do it as *you*.

CHAPTER 1: COMPLETE OPTIMIZATION

"Now to Him who is able to do immeasurably more than all we ask or imagine, according to His power that is at work within us." Ephesians 3:20

Introduction: The Power of Optimization

When it comes to pursuing our dreams, one of the most crucial things we can do is build a system that keeps us grounded and focused. True success isn't about short bursts of energy; it's about the daily habits and consistent actions that compound over time. Creating a system that integrates seamlessly into your life will make it easier to maintain motivation and stay on course, even when challenges arise.

The legendary industrialist Henry Ford once said, "Whether you think you can or think you can't, you're right." Ford's success was built not just on his skills or ideas, but on the system he created to support those ideas. When you believe you can and have a system that reinforces that belief, incredible things happen.

My Journey: Learning the Power of Focus

When I first started my journey as an entrepreneur, I was full of excitement. I wanted to share everything I was learning. I dove in headfirst, pouring my energy into speaking, coaching, training, podcasting, creating courses, and even affiliate marketing. I couldn't wait to make an impact and help others grow.

But there was a challenge: I was still in the military, and even though I dedicated my personal time to my business, some people didn't see it that way. One person, in particular, seemed determined to make my life difficult, questioning my intentions and even trying to get me in trouble. It wasn't easy. There were moments when I questioned whether it was worth the effort. But the adversity only fueled my commitment. I kept pushing forward, inspiring my team to win awards and mentoring others to reach new levels of success. I realized that adding value to others was what mattered most to me.

During this time, I also learned the importance of focus. While I was trying to do ten things at once, I realized that juggling so many ventures was holding me back from making a real impact. It was time to focus on one main thing and do it well. This decision not only strengthened my purpose but also helped me create a system that allowed me to serve others more effectively.

The Pillars of Complete Optimization

Complete Optimization means creating a system that supports you in every area of your life. It's about setting yourself up for success by taking care of the essentials: your environment, your health, and your mindset. Here's how you can start optimizing different aspects of your life to support your dreams.

Step 1: Power Up – Optimize Your Health

"Do you not know that your bodies are temples of the

Holy Spirit, who is in you, whom you have received from

God? You are not your own."

1 Corinthians 6:19

Success requires energy, mental, emotional, and physical. One of the most powerful things you can do is prioritize your health. This isn't about an all-or-nothing approach; it's about small, consistent changes that boost your energy levels and mental clarity.

Let me tell you a story. A few years ago, I was attending a conference with my friend Dr. Kenisha L. Williams. She's someone you'd describe as "Ms. Energy" always vibrant, always focused. But what struck me wasn't just her energy it was the discipline behind it. She shared with me that in order to show up as her best self, she couldn't just eat whatever was served at the conference. She actually researched healthy places to pick up food before arriving.

I asked her if that kind of discipline was hard. Her response? "It's not discipline. It's love and compassion."

That moment changed the way I viewed self-care. I realized I wasn't treating the future version of myself with that kind of compassion. But when I began fueling myself mentally, physically, and spiritually, I gained clarity and strength. If you want to show up with power, it starts with leading your mind and body first. The best DISC Alignment C-type personality.

Action Steps:

Daily: Choose one simple health habit to incorporate, drink more water, move your body, or fuel yourself with better food.

Weekly: Reflect on how you feel after a week of small health changes. Adjust as needed.

Step 2: Create a Motivational Environment

"Let all things be done decently and in order." 1

Corinthians 14:40

Your environment plays a big role in your ability to stay focused and inspired. Set up a workspace or corner in your home that feels motivating and energizing.

When I first started my business, I thought being productive meant being busy. I was taking in every podcast, every course, every quote, and my desk was buried in notes. But my mind felt scattered. The truth? I didn't need more information. I needed clarity. I began to realize that my environment wasn't reflecting my goals; it was mirroring my confusion. So I cleared my desk. I posted my top 3 goals. I hung a quote that reminded me of my purpose. And something shifted. I felt peace, focus, and momentum. The best DISC Alignment S-type personality.

Action Steps:

Daily: Tidy your workspace and add something inspiring.

Weekly: Add one motivational item or remove something that distracts you.

Step 3: Keep Your Gas Tank Full

"Come to me, all you who are weary and burdened, and I will give you rest." Matthew 11:28

Just as a car needs fuel, you need moments of rest and rejuvenation. Without proper breaks, burnout becomes inevitable.

I've had seasons where I was doing all the things, showing up for my business, my family, my commitments; however, deep down, I felt off. I was running on fumes. I'd go days feeling uninspired and disconnected. And then I remembered a lesson from my childhood, walking to the beach with my grandma. She'd sit on the back steps with her coffee and cigar after making me breakfast. As a kid, I thought, "Wow, Grandma's a boss." But looking back, I see now she was modeling peace, routine, and intentional rest. That was her fuel. And it taught me that success includes stillness. The best DISC Alignment I-type personality.

Action Steps:

Daily: Schedule short breaks. Do one thing that gives you joy or peace.

Weekly: Ask yourself: Where do I need to refuel? Then do it on purpose.

Step 4: Make Your Goals Visible

"Where there is no vision, the people perish: but he that keepeth the law, happy is he." Proverbs 29:18

If your goals are hidden in the back of your mind or buried under a pile of tasks, it's harder to stay focused. Find ways to keep them visible in your daily life.

When I was 19, I went to a Stephen Covey leadership conference and heard something that stuck: "Write your goals down and date them." So I did. I wrote three big goals on an envelope labeled, "Do not open until age 30." I achieved them all by 25. That envelope still sits in my office, not just as a reminder but as proof that when you put vision on paper, momentum follows. When my wife opened that envelope with me, she smiled and said, "You did it." And I remember thinking, "I could've dreamed even bigger." So now I do. The best DISC Alignment D-type personality.

Action Steps:

Daily: Write down your top goal and keep it visible.

Weekly: Review your progress. Stretch your faith. And if you're ready, write a few goals and tuck them into your own envelope.

Reflection Prompt

What's one optimization you could implement today that would make you feel more focused and organized?

What system or habit currently supports your goals, and where can you improve?

When have you felt overwhelmed by too many commitments? What did you learn, and how can you simplify your focus?

What one small change today could improve your energy, environment, or mindset?

Jose Transformational Story

A few years ago, I was mentoring a young leader who had all the ambition in the world, but he was stuck. He had vision but no energy, goals but no clarity. I remember him telling me, "I feel like I'm moving in circles." So we sat down and I asked him to walk me through his day. He admitted to skipping meals, staying up late, working in a cluttered space, and trying to juggle his vision with no time to breathe. He had no energy, no plan, and no room to think.

We didn't overhaul everything overnight. We started small, adding a simple morning walk, clearing just one drawer of his desk, carving out 30 minutes of stillness, and posting one visible goal on his mirror. That's it. But within just a few weeks, something shifted. He began to speak with more clarity. His energy returned. And instead of staying busy, he started making real progress. Three months later, he sent me a message that said, "I've never felt this focused in my life. I didn't realize how much my environment and habits were draining me." That moment stuck with me. Because the truth is, success doesn't always come from grinding harder. It comes from being more aligned. When your body, mind, space, and vision are working together, momentum isn't forced; it flows.

Bringing It All Together:

The Power of Optimization

Complete Optimization isn't about perfection; it's about building a system that supports you. It's about treating your life and future with enough love and intention that you build sustainable momentum. You can't build a dream from a depleted place, a scattered space, or with hidden goals. It's time to align your energy, your environment, and your focus. Every small step you take in that direction multiplies. Momentum is created by clarity. And clarity starts with caring enough to optimize how you show up.

Accelerate Your Success: Implementation Exercise

At the end of each chapter, you'll find an exercise to help you put these ideas into action. It's essential that you optimize every area of your life; however, you don't need to do it all at once. Find one you can implement daily or weekly and start there.

What three things can you implement and optimize right now?

_____

_____

_____

What three things do you need to optimize over time?

_____

_____

_____

What three things can you share with someone to stay accountable?

_____

_____

_____

Final Reflection:

Your Journey to Complete Optimization

Complete Optimization isn't about perfection; it's about building a system that supports you. By making small, consistent changes, you'll notice a shift in how you feel and how you approach your goals. Each small action compounds over time, creating momentum and making the journey more sustainable.

CHAPTER 2: LEAVING YOUR COMFORT ZONE

"Be strong and courageous. Do not be afraid or terrified because of them, for the Lord your God goes with you..."

Deuteronomy 31:6

Introduction: Growth Begins at the Edge

Leaving your comfort zone can feel like a big leap, but it's where growth really happens. Whether we're starting a new venture, trying a different approach, or taking on a challenge that feels intimidating, stepping into the unknown is often the quickest path to transformation. Embracing discomfort is a skill you can strengthen over time by pushing your boundaries just a bit every day.

As John Maxwell says, "You have to be comfortable with being uncomfortable." It's about learning to see challenges as opportunities to become the person you need to be to reach your dreams.

When I started my journey in the military, I had no idea how much it would teach me about stepping outside of my comfort zone. I found that each new role or responsibility stretched me in ways I hadn't anticipated. My desire to make a difference in others' lives became a guiding force, pushing me beyond what felt safe or comfortable.

As I balanced military responsibilities with my growing passion for speaking, coaching, and mentoring others, I encountered pushback. There were people who questioned my intentions, and some even tried to make it difficult for me to pursue my calling. But I realized that I couldn't let the opinions or actions of others define my path. I had to keep moving forward and trust that each step, no matter how uncomfortable, was building my character and helping me fulfill my purpose.

Through these experiences, I learned the value of persistence and found that every time I chose to lean into discomfort, I grew stronger and more confident. I discovered that purpose often reveals itself when we're willing to take risks and move beyond what feels safe.

The Pillars of Leaving Your Comfort Zone

Leaving your comfort zone is about making small, intentional choices to stretch beyond what feels easy. It's not about diving into overwhelming challenges right away but gradually building confidence through achievable steps that push your limits. The more you practice stepping out, the more resilient and adaptable you become.

Step 1: Be a Doer, Not Just a Thinker

"But be doers of the word, and not hearers only, deceiving yourselves." James 1:22

Back in 2017, I was fired up to start my entrepreneurial journey. I had just heard my mentor say something that shifted everything: "Make sure you're not just leaving something; focus on going to something." It was perfect timing because I was trying to decide whether or not to retire from the military.

The easy thing would've been to coast—to do what I had seen so many others do. What I called "ROAD" status: Retired On Active Duty. Just showing up. Doing the minimum. Waiting it out. But that wasn't me. I was built differently. Even without a title or position, I wanted to make a difference.

Still, I was torn. Do I keep pushing for promotion? Or do I take a risk and build something that could impact others? Then I asked myself a question that changed everything: "What if there's a third option?" What if... instead of chasing promotion or starting a business just for myself, I focused on helping others walk in their purpose with my business?

So I started sharing what I was learning, business ideas, leadership insights, and personal growth tools. But then the thoughts started creeping in: "Who do you think you are?" "Why would anyone listen to you?" "You're not even..." I let those thoughts paralyze me for about three months. I kept thinking. Overthinking. But not doing.

That's when I had to remind myself: Be a doer. Not just a thinker. Because thoughts don't build legacies, actions do. And as Jalen Hurts said, "I had a purpose before others had an opinion of me." That quote still gives me chills. Because if I had waited for validation, I'd still be waiting. Purpose doesn't need permission. The best DISC Alignment D-type personality.

Action Steps:

Daily: Choose one small step you can take today toward a goal that's outside your comfort zone.

Weekly: Reflect on the actions you took that stretched your boundaries.

Step 2: Use FIDO – Forget It and Drive On

"But one thing I do: Forgetting what is behind and straining toward what is ahead..." Philippians 3:13

Leadership isn't always about the big moments. Sometimes, it's in the quiet choices, doing what's right when it's easier to stay silent. A few years ago, a young lady came to me seeking mentorship. She was looking for guidance on a specific item, and I felt like it was the right moment to support her. I didn't just give her advice, I provided an example and even a template she could use. She left encouraged, equipped, and empowered.

But not long after, I was approached by her section lead. She wasn't happy. She told me I had no business helping her troop. That I was interfering. That I should've sent the young lady back to her. Honestly, I was caught off guard. My first thought? I didn't even know you were her section lead. My second? Isn't this what leaders are supposed to do? Help. Support. Equip.

This created unnecessary tension, and for a moment, I questioned whether I had overstepped. But then I remembered: "Leadership is about action, not position." When your intention is to add value, not take control, then helping isn't wrong.

Still… I had a choice to make. I could carry the offense and frustration, or I could release it, learn from it, and move on. So that's what I did. FIDO. Forget it… and drive on. Not because it didn't matter, but because staying stuck would've slowed me down from what mattered more. The best DISC Alignment S-type personality.

Action Steps:

Daily: Choose one thing to release today a fear, a mistake, or a misunderstanding.

Weekly: Reflect on moments of discouragement and how you reframed them.

Step 3: Small Wins, Strong Confidence

"Whoever can be trusted with very little can also be trusted with much..." Luke 16:10

One of the biggest challenges I ever accepted was when I made the intentional decision to grow as a leader. I sat down with my mentor, who was the senior leader over the location where I was assigned. He told me something that shifted everything: "If you want to become a better leader... start leading people who don't have to follow you." He wasn't talking about rank. He was talking about influence leading in places where people follow because of vision, not obligation.

So I stepped into a volunteer leadership role and brought the team together. We committed to hosting monthly events to develop leaders, running quarterly fundraisers to expand our reach, and setting a bold financial goal aligned with our purpose. We didn't just talk about vision, we broke it into micro-goals. One event at a time.

One strategy at a time. One win at a time. That's what built momentum. That's what built confidence not just in me, but in the entire team.

The result? We became the largest organization in membership. We exceeded our financial goals. And most importantly, we developed leaders who won awards at the highest level. Here's what I've learned: you don't build confidence by dreaming big. You build confidence by consistent action. Clarity fuels action. Micro-goals build belief. And when you move with focus, you grow with power. The best DISC Alignment C-type personality.

Action Steps:

Daily: Set one micro-goal each morning related to stepping outside your comfort zone.

Weekly: Review your progress and identify your next micro-step.

Step 4: Reframe the Moment, Reclaim the Mission

"And we know that in all things God works for the good of those who love him..." Romans 8:28

A few years ago, I was leading a fundraising event with a team I cared deeply about. We had the right strategy, the right product, the right price. But as the event began, other teams started selling similar products for cheaper. My team started to panic. I encouraged them: "Do you believe in the value of what we offer?" Everyone said yes. So we stuck to the plan. We added samples. Highlighted quality. Trusted our strategy.

Then came the twist... I stepped away briefly to attend church. When I came back, I found out the team had dropped the price, without consulting me or getting committee approval. I wasn't upset they changed the price. I was disappointed they didn't talk to me. Because I believe in team leadership. I value communication. I take ownership.

And honestly, in that moment, I felt like I failed. Not because we sold less (we actually sold out early). But I felt like I lost the connection with my team. But here's what I learned: failure isn't just about what goes wrong. It's about how we respond when something goes off course.

I had a choice to carry disappointment or extract direction. I chose to reframe it. We debriefed. We talked through the breakdown. And from that "failure" came one of the strongest seasons of team unity and leadership growth I've ever seen. The best DISC Alignment I-type personality.

Action Steps:

Daily: Write down one lesson from something that didn't go as planned.

Weekly: Reflect on what didn't work, and how it shaped your growth.

Reflection Prompts

What's one area of your life where you feel ready to stretch beyond your comfort zone?

What is one small step you can take today that feels challenging but manageable?

How can you use past failures as stepping stones for growth?

Chaunte Lowe's Resiliency Story

A powerful example of resilience and stepping out of one's comfort zone comes from my friend Chaunte Lowe, a four-time Olympic high jumper. After being diagnosed with breast cancer, she faced the most difficult period of her life. She had to step away from her sport and focus on her health. This time of discomfort allowed her to reconnect with her purpose and find inner strength.

Her journey highlights that sometimes stepping away from comfort is about letting go of what we know to discover new depths of resilience. Even though she didn't make it to the 2020 Olympics due to COVID-19, her journey was about more than medals. It was about inspiring others and showing the power of pushing through discomfort, even in the face of life's hardest challenges.

Bringing It All Together:

Building Resilience Through Discomfort

Leaving your comfort zone isn't something you do once; it's something you practice over time. Each small step builds resilience, each setback teaches you a lesson, and each victory strengthens your resolve. Growth doesn't happen overnight, but by intentionally stretching yourself each day, you can create a life that's not only successful but deeply fulfilling.

Accelerate Your Success: Implementation Exercise

At the end of each chapter, you'll find an exercise to help you put these ideas into action. Success comes from taking consistent, intentional steps each day.

What three things can you implement right now to push yourself outside your comfort zone?

_____

_____

_____

What three things do you need to implement over time to build resilience?

_____

_____

_____

What three things can you share with someone to stay accountable?

_____

_____

_____

Final Reflection:

Embracing Discomfort as a Path to Growth

Leaving your comfort zone is an ongoing journey. Each time you step into the unknown, you're not only strengthening yourself but also opening doors to opportunities you never imagined. The discomfort you face today is building the resilience you'll rely on tomorrow. Remember, growth lies just beyond the edges of what feels comfortable; embrace it, and watch yourself transform.

CHAPTER 3: EMBRACING MISTAKES

"Though the righteous fall seven times, they rise again."

Proverbs 24:16

Introduction: The Power of Embracing Mistakes

One of the most important lessons on the journey to success is realizing that mistakes aren't failures; they're steps forward. Mistakes show us what doesn't work and help us refine our approach. They build resilience, deepen our understanding, and ultimately propel us closer to our goals. To truly progress, you have to give yourself permission to make mistakes, learn from them, and keep moving forward.

As Michael Jordan once said, "I've missed more than 9,000 shots in my career. I've lost almost 300 games. Twenty-six times, I've been trusted to take the game-winning shot and missed. I've failed over and over and over again in my life. And that is why I succeed."

My Journey: Mistakes as Stepping Stones

Starting my business wasn't a smooth journey; it was filled with mistakes. When I first launched, I tried to do too much all at once: speaking, coaching, creating courses, affiliate marketing, and even podcasting. I figured, "How hard could it be?" I saw big names doing it and thought I could too. But I was looking at their gifts, their teams, their success, not realizing it was just me behind the scenes. I poured energy into too many areas and couldn't make a real impact in any of them. At first, I could have seen it as a failure. But instead, I chose to see it as a signpost. That season taught me that success doesn't come from doing everything; it comes from doing the right things well. Every mistake pointed me toward clarity. Focus. Excellence. And impact.

The Pillars of Embracing Mistakes

Embracing mistakes means reframing how you see failure. Instead of viewing mistakes as setbacks, see them as stepping stones that bring you closer to success. Each mistake carries a lesson, and each lesson makes you stronger, wiser, and more prepared for the future.

Step 1: Take Purposeful Risks to Grow

"Commit to the Lord whatever you do, and He will establish your plans." Proverbs 16:3

When I decided to host my first big solo leadership event, I was fueled by passion. I wanted to help people. I wanted to make a difference. I poured everything I had into it, booked the venue, built the content, and promoted it with all my heart. The amazing part? We sold out. The humbling part? I made nothing. Why? Because I forgot to build a real budget. I didn't allocate costs or factor in expenses like a smart business leader should. From a financial standpoint, it was a loss. But from a leadership lens? It was one of the best growth moments of my life. The feedback was phenomenal. The impact was real. And I realized that passion without stewardship isn't sustainable. Mistakes are often the tuition we pay for wisdom. The best DISC Alignment D-type personality.

Action Steps:

Daily: Take one small risk that stretches your comfort zone.

Weekly: Reflect on what it taught you and how it will shape your next decision.

Step 2: Practice "Press On" Thinking

"Not that I have already obtained all this... but I press on to take hold of that for which Christ Jesus took hold of me." Philippians 3:12

When I stepped into my first medical leadership role, I assumed it would be simple. After all, I had experience leading large teams and high-stakes missions. But this team was different; it was small, diverse, and deeply human. One day, while we were working at the front desk, the youngest team member made a disrespectful comment. I corrected them privately, and I thought respectfully. But the cultural lens was different. What I saw as grace, they experienced as shame. That moment changed me. I could've brushed it off and said, "They'll get over it." Instead, I leaned in and asked, "How could I grow?" I realized leadership isn't just about intention; it's about impact. Failing forward means allowing your mistakes to sharpen you, not shame you. That's what "pressing on" looks like: not avoiding the hard stuff, but learning from it. The best DISC Alignment S-type personality.

Action Steps:

Daily: Record a lesson from anything that didn't go to plan.

Weekly: Review and ask, "How can I grow from this?"

"Do not despise these small beginnings, for the Lord

rejoices to see the work begin..." Zechariah 4:10

Early in my career, I thought only the big moments mattered-promotions, awards, recognition. But I overlooked how the small wins shape our story. And the small failures? They sharpen our character. I remember walking through what felt like one of the worst season of my life. I didn't get the promotion I worked hard for. My grandmother had just passed. I felt like I was failing-like none of it mattered. Then out of nowhere, I got a call: someone wanted to interview me for a success magazine. I thought, "What? Now?" It felt so opposite of what

I was walking through. But as we spoke, he reminded me: "You've had a successful career that's just getting started. You've been married for over ten years. You're raising amazing kids. You're making an impact even when it doesn't feel like it." That conversation shifted everything. I learned that if you don't pause to celebrate the small wins, you'll miss the progress happening right under your feet. And if you don't reflect on the small failures, you'll miss the growth hidden inside of them. The best DISC Alignment C-type personality.

Action Steps:

Daily: Celebrate one win, even if it's small.

Weekly: Reflect on one failure and what it taught you.

Step 4: Shift Your Perspective

"The Lord makes firm the steps of the one who delights in him; though he may stumble, he will not fall, for the Lord upholds him with his hand." Psalm 37:23-24

One of the most freeing moments in my journey was learning that mistakes aren't losses, they're lessons. They're not roadblocks, they're redirections. When I launched my business, I tried to mimic everything I saw from leaders I admired. Speaking. Coaching. Courses.

Content. Affiliate marketing. Podcasting. I tried to do it all, but I had none of their infrastructure or support. I was running five races at once alone. Eventually, I realized: trying to be everything to everyone would keep me from making a real impact with anyone. That wasn't a failure. That was the turning point. When you let go of trying to do it all, you give yourself permission to grow where you're truly called. The biggest lessons are often wrapped inside our boldest missteps. The best DISC Alignment, I-type personality.

Action Steps:

Daily: Ask yourself, "What is this teaching me?"

Weekly: Track your lessons and apply one forward.

What's one mistake you made recently that taught you a valuable lesson?

How can you apply that lesson to your next step?

What small goal feels like a healthy stretch right now?

Story of Transformation:

Peter's Journey of Accountability and Redemption

Peter's story is a powerful example of how mentorship can turn a painful moment into a purposeful mission. Long before the breakthrough, Peter asked me to mentor him. He wanted accountability. Growth. Change. And we both agreed to walk that journey together. Then came the unexpected: a DUI.

It was a hard moment, one with real consequences. But what struck me most was Peter's response. He didn't run from it. He didn't make excuses. Instead, he came to me with humility and said, "If you want to end the mentorship, I understand." He was honoring the fact that

I had a choice. But my choice was simple. Despite what I was going through in my own life, I knew I had made a commitment not just to mentor Peter, but to walk in the purpose God placed in me: to bring the best out of others, no matter what they've been through. So I stayed. And so did he. Peter took full ownership of his mistake. He didn't just want a second chance; he wanted to become the kind of man who lived with integrity. Together, we focused not on what he lost, but on what he could rebuild.

And rebuild, he did.

He began speaking to others about the dangers of drinking and driving, using his pain to prevent theirs. Every time he shared his story, it wasn't just a warning; it was a witness. He became living proof that accountability isn't weakness, it's strength. That failure doesn't disqualify you; it refines you.

Peter's courage reminded me that mistakes don't cancel your purpose; they clarify it. And with the right support, your failure can become someone else's freedom. His story also reminded me that mentorship isn't about being perfect; it's about choosing to believe in someone even when life gets messy. And honoring that belief with action. Because when someone chooses to rise, and you choose to walk with them, you both grow stronger in the process.

Bringing It All Together:

Building Confidence Through Mistakes

Mistakes aren't the enemy. They're the education. Each time you fall and rise, you build deeper confidence. Not just in your abilities, but in your character. Success isn't found in perfection-it's built in persistence. Let your mistakes teach you, stretch you, and shape the future you're building.

What three things can you implement right now to overcome the fear of making mistakes?

_____

_____

_____

What three things do you need to implement over time to build resilience through mistakes?

_____

_____

_____

What three things can you share with someone to stay accountable as do you embrace mistakes as part of your journey?

_____

_____

_____

Final Reflection: Growing Through Mistakes

Mistakes are powerful teachers. Don't let fear silence your growth. Every misstep has meaning. Every fall can lead to forward motion. The sooner you embrace your mistakes, the faster you'll discover what's possible.

CHAPTER 4: MASTERING SELFTALK

"Whatever is true, whatever is noble, whatever is right...

think about such things." Philippians 4:8

Introduction: The Power of Self-Talk

The conversations you have with yourself are some of the most important ones you'll ever have. What we say to ourselves shapes our actions, our beliefs, and ultimately, our lives. When we let negative self-talk dominate, it creates doubt, fear, and hesitation. But when we intentionally practice positive self-talk, it fosters resilience, confidence, and a growth-oriented mindset. Learning to talk to yourself instead of listening to the doubts or fears that might arise is a critical step on the path to success.

As Proverbs 23:7 says, "For as he thinks in his heart, so is he." This verse reminds us that our inner thoughts define us. By changing how we talk to ourselves, we can change the way we see ourselves and what we believe is possible.

When I first started pursuing my dreams, I faced the same doubts that many people do. Questions like, "What if I fail?" or "Am I really capable of this?" would creep in, especially in challenging moments. It was easy to let those voices create doubt and hesitation, but I realized that if I kept listening to them, they'd hold me back.

To change my mindset, I began practicing positive affirmations daily. Every morning, I would repeat affirmations that aligned with my goals, reminding myself of my purpose and potential. Instead of letting doubt speak the loudest, I decided to talk to myself with confidence, and over time, those affirmations became my truth. This practice helped me push through challenges and gave me the strength to pursue my calling wholeheartedly.

Mastering self-talk is about learning to speak to yourself with encouragement, reminding yourself of your strengths and focusing on possibilities rather than limitations. When you practice positive self-talk consistently, it helps you cultivate a mindset that's resilient, optimistic, and open to growth.

Step 1: Replace Doubts with Affirmations

"So is my word that goes out from my mouth: It will not return to me empty, but will accomplish what I desire..."

Isaiah 55:11

When I first started writing this book, I wrestled with the same doubts that try to stop most of us. Thoughts like, "Who's going to care what I have to say?" "What if I'm not qualified enough?" and "What if I fail in front of everyone?" kept looping in my mind. I didn't need another motivational quote, I needed to reprogram my mindset. That's when I made a decision: I would no longer give doubt the final word in my life. Every time a negative thought showed up, I started answering back with the truth. I replaced self-doubt with affirmations rooted in experience, faith, and vision: "I was called for this." "I've been prepared through every challenge I've faced." "What I have is valuable, and someone needs it." It didn't happen overnight. But one shift at a time, my inner dialogue started to sound more like my future, and less like my fear. That's what this step is all about: rewiring your self-talk so that belief leads the way. Speak what you want to grow into. Speak what you want to see take root. Your words are the blueprint. Build wisely. The best DISC Alignment I-type personality.

Action Steps:

Daily Action: Start each morning with one empowering affirmation that aligns with your goals. Write it down, say it out loud, and keep it with you throughout the day.

Weekly Action: Reflect on your affirmations for the week. Did any particular affirmation resonate strongly? How did it impact your mindset or actions?

Step 2: Identify and Challenge Limiting Beliefs

"Let God transform you into a new person by changing the way you think." Romans 12:2

Before I ever got paid to speak or coach... before I launched a business or stood on a stage with a mic in my hand... I already had years of experience under my belt. But when I stepped out to do it on my own, no rank, no uniform, no structure behind me, something strange happened. That's when doubt crept in. "Are you really ready for this?" "What if no one sees your value?" "What if this doesn't work?" "Who are you to do this?" "You've never done it like this before." It wasn't because I lacked the experience. The military gave me plenty of opportunities to speak, train, coach, and lead. I had led teams. I had mentored countless individuals. I had spoken in front of groups big and small, not because I had to, but because I wanted to make an impact.

So why was I doubting myself now? Because this time, it felt different. This time, I wasn't operating under a job title. This time it was my name, my message, my vision. Let me repeat that, my name. And that's when I realized: the fear wasn't about my ability. It was about the unknown. It was about stepping into something new and unfamiliar. And fear loves to show up when we're doing something we've never done before.

But here's what changed everything for me: I stopped just listening to the fear. And I started talking back. I reminded myself, "This isn't your first time speaking." "This isn't your first time leading or coaching." "This is just the first time you're doing it under your own brand, and that's OK." The conversation I had to start having with myself was simple: "You're not starting from zero, you're starting from experience." "You've done this before, just in a different context." "The call didn't start with the business. The business came from the call." That shift in my inner conversation made all the difference.

As 2 Corinthians 10:5 says, we must take every thought captive and make it obedient to Christ. That means we don't just passively accept fear-based thinking—we confront it, challenge it, and replace it with truth. If you think small, you'll lead small. If you think scared, you'll act stuck. But if you believe you're called and equipped, you'll walk in that belief. The beliefs we hold shape the actions we take. So when fear shows up, don't let it drive the car. Talk back with truth. Speak life over your mission. And remind yourself, you're not starting from scratch. You're starting from experience. The best DISC Alignment C-type personality.

Action Steps:

Daily Action: Take a moment to notice any negative or self-limiting thoughts. Write them down, then challenge each one by asking, "Is this really true? What's a more empowering belief I could hold instead?"

Weekly Action: Review your limiting beliefs and the new empowering beliefs you've created. How can you continue to replace old beliefs with new ones that support your goals?

Step 3: Practice Self-Compassion

"As a father has compassion on his children, so the Lord has compassion on those who fear him."

Psalm 103: 13–14

There was a time in my life when I was doing a lot, building the business, trying to be a great husband, showing up for my kids, leading, speaking, coaching, and serving. And yet, anytime I fell short, even slightly, I'd be harder on myself than anyone else ever could be. I'd beat myself up mentally: "You should've handled that better." "Why are you still making this mistake?" "You've come too far to be slipping like this." On the outside, I was coaching others with grace. But on the inside, I had no grace for myself.

Then one day, I was talking to my son Deonte'. He was frustrated with himself about a game and how he performed. He was really hard on himself, more than I expected. I tried to reassure him. I told him it was okay, that one moment didn't define him. But no matter what I said, it didn't seem to land. Then it hit me... he couldn't grow because he wasn't giving himself grace, and I realized he learned that from me. Ouch!!!

It was like looking in a mirror. He had picked up the very pattern I had modeled for years. And now, even though I was trying to change, he had already inherited the habit. That moment became a turning point. Because I realized: this isn't just about me, it's about the legacy I'm leaving. If I wanted my son to lead himself with compassion, I had to start showing him how.

Because you can't grow in an environment of constant judgment. You can't raise strong leaders while modeling self-shame. And I asked myself, "Would I talk to someone I'm mentoring the way I talk to myself?" "What would happen if I led myself with the same patience I give others?" That's when everything started to shift. Self-compassion became a non-negotiable. Because real transformation doesn't happen through shame, it happens through grace, growth, and consistent self-respect. If you want to master the inner conversation, make sure that voice inside your head is one that builds, not breaks. Lead yourself with the kind of grace you want others to walk in. That's not weakness. That's leading yourself well. The best DISC Alignment S-type personality.

Action Steps:

Daily Action: When you make a mistake or feel discouraged, remind yourself that setbacks are a natural part of growth. Speak to yourself with the same compassion you would offer a friend.

Weekly Action: Reflect on moments when you practiced self-compassion. How did it impact your mood, mindset, or motivation? What's one way you can continue nurturing this compassionate approach?

Step 4: Visualize Success and Talk to Yourself

"I can do all this through him who gives me strength."

Philippians 4:13

There was a time I was asked to lead a mission trip to Peru. I wasn't supposed to be in charge. I had prepared to assist, to support, to serve. But just before we left, the lead doctor canceled due to a family emergency. Suddenly, the team turned to me: "Do you want to postpone the mission, or can you lead?"

At first, I was excited. It felt like a new opportunity. Then, just as quickly, insecurity crept in. "Are you sure you're ready?" "What if you mess this up?" "What if they realize you're not good enough to lead it alone?" Those thoughts hit me hard. But instead of backing down, I reminded myself of something a mentor once told me: "Learn as much as you can. Make it so clear and simple that the doctors feel like they don't even have to work."

That wisdom stuck with me. As soon as we arrived and the mission began, I stopped second-guessing. I stepped into the role—not with arrogance, but with alignment. I remembered my training. I remembered why I was there. I remembered who I was. I didn't try to overcompensate. I didn't pretend to be someone I wasn't. I just led with excellence and made it easy for whoever came after me to pick up where I left off.

In just seven days, we saw nearly 4,000 people. I documented every detail, prepared every patient for the next phase of care, and did it all with confidence, not because I had a title, but because I knew my identity. That trip reminded me: you don't need a title to lead. You don't need applause to show up fully. You don't need to wait for permission to operate in your assignment. Speak from identity, not insecurity. You've been prepared for more than you realize. You've learned more than you think. And when the moment comes, you'll be ready, because you already are. The best DISC Alignment D-type personality.

Action Steps:

Daily Action: Take a few minutes each day to visualize yourself achieving a specific goal. See it as clearly as possible, and mentally talk yourself through any challenges you may face along the way.

Weekly Action: Reflect on your visualization practice. Did you feel more prepared or confident in certain situations? How can you use visualization to stay connected to your vision?

Reflection Prompts

These prompts are designed to help you assess your self-talk and strengthen positive inner dialogue:

What's one belief you've held about yourself that you're ready to change?

What is one empowering affirmation that you can start using daily to build confidence?

How can you practice self-compassion in moments of doubt or frustration?

Story of Transformation:

Kristan's Journey to Confidence

I remember having a deep conversation with my friend Kristan about confidence. We were talking about how easy it is to encourage others, yet how hard it can be to speak that same belief over ourselves. That's when she shared a story with me that really stuck.

Kristan had always been passionate about leadership. But one day, she was asked by a client, PNG, to deliver a presentation on *The Confidence Code.* At first, she smiled at the opportunity, but as the day got closer, she told me she started to feel that familiar wave of doubt. *Am I really the right person to speak on this?* The irony wasn't lost on her she was about to teach confidence while silently battling her own.

Rather than backing down, Kristan made a choice. She shifted her self-talk. She replaced the fear with truth: *I have experience. I am prepared. I belong in this room.* She started visualizing the presentation before it even happened, seeing herself stand strong, speak clearly, and deliver value with impact. She told me that was the turning point. When the day finally arrived, something clicked inside her. As she began speaking, it wasn't just theory it was her own transformation in real time. The more she taught, the more she believed. By the end of the session, it was clear: she hadn't just taught on confidence she had walked it out.

That moment changed everything for Kristan. And for me, too. Because it reminded both of us that confidence isn't about never feeling fear. It's about choosing to believe in yourself anyway. It's about mastering the inner conversation so that faith, not fear, leads the way.

Bringing It All Together:

Cultivating a Mindset of Resilience

Learning to talk to yourself positively is a daily practice that builds resilience over time. By replacing doubts with empowering affirmations, challenging limiting beliefs, and practicing self-compassion, you create a mindset that supports your goals. This habit not only strengthens your confidence but also prepares you to face any challenge with a clear and constructive inner dialogue.

Accelerate Your Success: Implementation Exercise

At the end of each chapter, you'll find an exercise to help you put these ideas into action. Your inner dialogue shapes your reality—take small, consistent steps to cultivate a positive mindset.

What three empowering affirmations can you start using daily to replace self-doubt?

_____

_____

_____

What three limiting beliefs can you work on challenging and replacing with constructive thoughts?

_____

_____

_____

What three visualization practices can help you stay connected to your goals?

_____

_____

_____

Final Reflection:

Shaping Your Future Through Self-Talk

The words you speak to yourself shape your life. Each time you choose an empowering thought over a limiting belief, you're building a foundation for success. Remember, self-talk isn't just about positive thinking— it's about creating an inner dialogue that aligns with who you're becoming. Embrace the power of talking to yourself instead of listening to the doubts, and you'll find yourself moving forward with clarity, confidence, and purpose.

CHAPTER 5: YOUR MOST VALUABLE ASSET

"Love your neighbor as yourself." Matthew 22:39

Introduction: The Power of Self-Investment

One of the greatest realizations you can have on the path to success is understanding that your most valuable asset is you, your skills, your strengths, and your unique perspective. When you recognize and invest in your own potential, you create a foundation for long-term growth and fulfillment. Success doesn't just happen; it's the result of continuous self-investment, learning, and growth.

As author and speaker Jim Rohn said, "Investing in yourself is the best investment you will ever make. It will not only improve your life, it will improve the lives of all those around you." This chapter is about embracing your value, nurturing your talents, and building a mindset that sees personal growth as essential to achieving your goals.

My Journey: Discovering the Power of Self-Worth

Throughout my career, I faced moments of doubt—times when I questioned my abilities or whether I was "enough" to reach my goals. But every time I invested in learning, mentoring, or refining my skills, I discovered a deeper capacity within myself. I realized that my potential was limitless, as long as I believed in it and put in the work to develop it.

When I began to view myself as my most valuable asset, everything changed. I stopped waiting for external validation and instead focused on personal growth. This shift empowered me to take on challenges with confidence, knowing that my commitment to learning and self-improvement was building a strong foundation for success.

The Pillars of Self-Worth and Investment

Recognizing your own value is the first step; the next is actively investing in yourself. This means dedicating time and resources to develop your strengths, build new skills, and deepen your self-belief. When you see yourself as worthy of investment, you unlock the potential to achieve more than you ever imagined.

Step 1: Identify Your Strengths and Passions

"We have different gifts, according to the grace given to each of us..." Romans 12:6 (NIV)

For years, I poured into others as a mentor, a leader, and a coach. But early in my entrepreneurial journey, I had to ask myself a hard question: When was the last time I truly invested in myself? Not the version of me wearing the uniform... not the one helping others grow... but the real me the one who still had purpose to pursue, areas to grow, and goals to reach.

It's easy to invest in things that make us look successful suits, shoes, cars, business cards, websites, logos. But what about the things that build your character, sharpen your skills, and stretch your mindset? The books. The coaching. The deep conversations. The uncomfortable breakthroughs.

There came a moment when I realized: I am my most valuable asset. And if I didn't start treating myself that way, I'd burn out trying to build everyone else.

So I got honest. I looked at where I was strong, what I was passionate about, and what gave me energy. And I started pouring into that.

It wasn't flashy. It wasn't overnight. But it was solid. I joined Maxwell Leadership. I started attending business masterminds. I became part of the Unleashed U community. I even attended marriage and men's retreats because I wanted to become a better husband, not just a better leader.

That internal investment started producing external results. Because when you believe in your own value, you stop looking around for someone to validate your dream, and you start building from the inside out.

"You're not just a business or a brand. You are an asset, and your life reflects how well you steward that asset. So invest wisely. Protect your energy. Own your growth. Because everything connected to you grows when you do. The best DISC Alignment I type personality.

Action Steps:

Daily Action: Take a few minutes each day to reflect on moments when you felt engaged, energized, or fulfilled. These moments often reveal your strengths.

Weekly Action: Write down three strengths or skills you value most in yourself. Set a goal to nurture one of these areas by learning or practicing something new in the upcoming week.

Step 2: Set Aside Time for Self-Improvement

"Do your best to present yourself to God as one approved, a worker who does not need to be ashamed..."

2 Timothy 2:15

One of the biggest lies I believed early on was this: "When things slow down... when I get to a certain level... then I'll invest in myself." But here's the truth: things rarely slow down, and the "right level" is a moving target.

I was juggling a lot. Trying to grow a business. Be present with my wife and kids. Serve others. Stay mission-minded.

I kept saying, "Once I get past this project... this event... this season..." Until one day I looked up and realized the calendar was always full. And yet, I didn't feel full. I was doing a lot, but I wasn't growing like I could have been.

But the real shift happened when I realized this: I was operating with backwards logic. I thought I needed to reach a certain level before I could invest. But that mindset? That's what I call stinking thinking and it'll sink your ship if you let it

Let me put it this way... When I was working toward my black belt, I didn't expect to earn the belt first and then pay my instructor. No I had to pay to learn. I had to invest in the training, the discipline, and the knowledge it took to become that next-level version of me.

Leadership and business are no different. Most people think, "Once I arrive, I'll invest." But the truth is, you have to invest in order to become that version of yourself.

So I started being intentional. I didn't just block out time, I blocked out priorities on my calendar. I scheduled time to read, pray, reflect, and grow. I also scheduled events I would attend for personal development, and events I would lead to add value to others, where I'd speak, coach, or train.

That calendar became a tool for alignment. And alignment is my guiding word for 2025. It reminded me: This isn't just about staying busy. It's about building. Becoming. Becoming better on purpose.

And when I started honoring those intentional blocks of time? Everything around me shifted. More clarity. More confidence. More consistency. Because growth doesn't happen by chance, it happens by choice. The best DISC Alignment C type personality.

Action Steps:

Daily Action: Dedicate at least ten minutes a day to a self-improvement activity, like reading a book, learning something new, or practicing a skill.

Weekly Action: Schedule a dedicated block of time each week for deeper learning or skill development. Reflect on what you gained from this time and how it supports your goals.

Step 3: Build a Support System for Growth

"Two are better than one... If either of them falls down, one can help the other up." Ecclesiastes 4:9–10

For a long time, I wore the badge of "I got it" like it was a medal of honor. I'll figure it out. I'll carry it. I'll lead it. I'll build it.

And in the military, that mindset served me, to a point. But in leadership and business, growth isn't a solo mission.

Eventually, I realized my own motivation was just the tip of the iceberg. I didn't need cheerleaders, I needed challengers. People who wouldn't let me play small. People who had high standards and helped me raise mine.

I had to be honest with myself about where I was, and even more honest about where I wanted to go.

That's when things started to shift.

I became intentional about who had access to my thoughts, my time, and my table. I joined mastermind groups. I leaned into the Unleashed U community. I built real friendships with leaders who were serious about their own growth.

And I also formed several business partnerships with both men and women I believe in, and trust. Partners who share my values, my vision, and the commitment to create lasting impact and meaningful change.

Here's what I've learned:

You can't rise higher while staying surrounded by voices that keep you comfortable.

Surround yourself with people who make you better not by flattering you, but by:

- Challenging you to get clear

- Encouraging you to take risks

- Being real with you when you need to make a shift

The right circle won't just hype you up, they'll help you grow. Build yourself an A-team. Because growth may start with you, but it's sustained and multiplied by who's walking with you. The best DISC Alignment S type personality.

Action Steps:

Daily Action: Reach out to someone in your network—a friend, mentor, or colleague—and ask for their perspective or advice on a current goal.

Weekly Action: Reflect on the impact of your interactions with supportive individuals. How has their encouragement or feedback helped you grow? Consider how you can also offer support to others on their journey.

Step 4: Create a Personal Development Plan

"Good planning and hard work lead to prosperity, but hasty shortcuts lead to poverty." Proverbs 21:5

There came a point in my journey where I had to get real honest: What do I want my life to look like? What do I want my business to look like? What do I want my family to look like?

I wasn't just thinking about success. I was thinking about legacy. I didn't want to live on autopilot. I wanted to live on purpose. But here's the thing: I wasn't handed a manual for any of it. Not for marriage. Not for business. Not for fatherhood. And I bet you weren't either.

And wishing for things to change? That wasn't an option.

Wishing doesn't build anything; intentionality does.

So I sat down and got serious. I started thinking about what I really wanted in every area of my life, and then I asked myself:

What do I need to do to create that? That's when I started building a personal development plan. I got clear on:

- The kind of husband, father, and leader I wanted to be

- The kind of business I wanted to run

- The kind of spiritual, mental, and emotional health I wanted to carry

Then I asked: What skills do I need to develop? What gaps do I need to close? What habits do I need to upgrade?

From there, I built a plan, simple but powerful:

- Clear goals

- Skill development priorities

- Books and training commitments

- Events and environments that stretch me

- Weekly time to reflect and recalibrate

And guess what? I stopped guessing whether I was growing because now I could track it. Like Dr. Stephen R. Covey once said, "Begin with the end in mind." And once I got clear on the end, the steps I needed to take started becoming obvious.

A vision without a plan is just a wish. But a plan with clarity, backed by purpose? That's how you build the life you were born to live. The best DISC Alignment D type personality.

Action Steps:

Daily Action: Write down one goal you're working toward and the skills or knowledge you need to achieve it. Break down a small step you can take today.

Weekly Action: Review your personal development plan. What progress have you made, and what adjustments are needed? Celebrate each milestone, no matter how small.

Reflection Prompts

Here are a few prompts to help you recognize your value and identify areas for growth:

What are three strengths you possess that you're proud of? How can you use them to reach your goals?

What is one area where you would like to invest more time in developing?

Who in your life supports your growth, and how can you lean on them for guidance or encouragement?

Story of Transformation:

MJ's Journey to Self-Worth and Growth

MJ had always been a dedicated and hardworking individual, but like many entrepreneurs, he struggled with self-doubt. As an immigrant from Cuba, he faced numerous challenges while building his businesses. He often felt the need for external validation to prove his worth, and while he had achieved success on the surface, deep down, he doubted his own abilities. This mindset limited him, keeping him from taking on new challenges or pursuing bigger goals.

One day, MJ decided to invest in himself, not just in his business skills but in personal growth as well. We both enrolled in personal development, joined a coaching program, and made a commitment to discovering our strengths. Over time, MJ realized that he had a wealth of talent, resilience, and strategic insight that he hadn't acknowledged before. By focusing on his own development, he unlocked a newfound confidence that allowed him to take bigger risks, expand his business ventures, and reach new heights in his career.

Today, MJ not only excels as a serial entrepreneur but also mentors others, helping them recognize their own value and potential. His journey demonstrates that investing in yourself can be the most powerful tool for personal and professional transformation.

Bringing It All Together:

Building a Mindset of Self-Worth

Recognizing and investing in your value is a lifelong journey. Each time you commit to learning, each time you build a skill, you're building a stronger foundation for success. By seeing yourself as your most valuable asset, you'll find the motivation to grow, the courage to take risks, and the confidence to pursue your dreams.

Accelerate Your Success: Implementation Exercise

At the end of each chapter, you'll find an exercise to help you put these ideas into action. Investing in yourself starts with small, intentional steps each day. Do it now, don't wait for someone else to do it.

What three strengths can you focus on developing to reach your goals?

_____

_____

_____

What three resources or activities can help you grow in areas important to your goals?

_____

_____

_____

What three people can you rely on for support or feedback as you pursue your growth journey?

_____

_____

_____

Final Reflection: Embracing Your Value

When you see yourself as worthy of investment, you unlock a new level of potential. Remember, growth doesn't happen overnight—it's a series of small, intentional actions that build over time. Embrace your value, believe in your potential, and commit to becoming the best version of yourself. You are your most valuable asset, and investing in yourself is the most rewarding journey you'll ever take.

CHAPTER 6: THE POWER SHIFT

"Mark out a straight path for your feet; stay on the safe path." Proverbs 4:26

Introduction: Taking Control of Your Life

One of the most transformative shifts you can make on the journey to success is moving from a reactive mindset to a proactive one. When we live reactively, we're always responding to what life throws at us, waiting for the "right" time, letting circumstances dictate our actions, and feeling like success is something outside of our control. But when we adopt a proactive mindset, we take ownership of our choices, focus on what we can control, and create momentum toward our goals.

As Stephen Covey said, "I am not a product of my circumstances. I am a product of my decisions." This chapter is about making that mental shift, stepping into the driver's seat of your life, choosing your direction, and acting with intention.

My Journey: Embracing the Power Shift

There was a time when I found myself in a cycle of reacting to life's demands. With responsibilities piling up, I felt like I was constantly playing catch-up, and it seemed like my goals were slipping out of reach. I realized that waiting for ideal circumstances to pursue my dreams was a road to nowhere. It became clear that I needed to take control and start making intentional choices if I wanted to achieve my vision.

By focusing on what I could control, my actions, my mindset, and my commitment to growth, I began to create my own path. I stopped letting setbacks define me and started viewing each obstacle as an opportunity to learn and improve. Embracing this power shift was one of the best decisions I ever made, and it's a decision you can make for yourself, too.

There was a season in my life when I found myself spiraling emotionally, not because of what was happening *in* me, but because of what I was trying to control *around* me. I remember sitting in my living room, recovering from an injury, and feeling this deep sense of guilt. The thought that kept echoing was, "I'm letting people down." But then a second thought came: "Wait... I'm healing. I'm doing everything I can. Why am I carrying guilt over something out of my control?" That was a lightbulb moment. I realized I had been giving too much energy to what others might think, and not enough to what I could actually influence. From that point on, I began managing my energy differently. I focused on my attitude, my effort, my recovery, and my mindset. That one shift helped me reclaim my sense of purpose not by doing more, but by doing what mattered most within my control.

Step 1: Identify What You Can Control

"Pay careful attention to your own work... For we are each responsible for our own conduct." Galatians 6: 4–5

There's a shift that happens in leadership and life when you realize: most of your power is in what you choose to focus on. Early on, I wasted a lot of energy trying to control things that were out of my hands: people's opinions, timing, outcomes, and how others showed up. And when those things didn't go the way I hoped, I would internalize it, take it personally, try harder, push more. But eventually, I burned out. Not because I wasn't passionate, but because I was mismanaging my power.

There was a season in my life when I found myself struggling emotionally, not because of what was happening in me, but because I was trying to control everything around me. I had just come out of surgery, and the silence was deafening. No speaking engagements. No coaching calls. No traveling. Just me, the couch, and the noise in my head. I remember lying there, ice pack on my leg, scrolling through social media and seeing others do everything I couldn't, and the guilt hit hard. I thought, "I'm falling behind. I'm letting people down." But then a new thought surfaced: "You're not falling behind. You're healing." That was a turning point. I had spent years measuring my worth by how much I could do for others. But in that moment, I realized I had to stop outsourcing my peace. I had to stop trying to win people's approval and start reclaiming my own presence. That was the beginning of the shift, learning to protect my energy, focus on my mindset, and live from purpose, not pressure. I couldn't control the healing speed. I couldn't control others' expectations. But I could control my attitude, my actions, and my attention. And that changed everything. The Best DISC Alignment C-type personality.

Action Steps:

Daily Action: Each day, identify one area where you're feeling stuck or frustrated. Ask yourself, "What part of this situation can I control?" and take one small action in that direction.

Weekly Action: Reflect on situations where focusing on what you could control made a positive difference. How can you apply this approach to other areas of your life?

Step 2: Set Clear Intentions for Your Day

"So teach us to number our days that we may get a heart of wisdom." Psalm 90:12

There was a time when I'd wake up, check my phone, and start... Emails. Notifications. Texts. Reacting. Other people's priorities set the tone for my day before I even took a breath. I felt productive... but not purposeful. I was busy... but not aligned. Most days, I'd get to work, move from meeting to meeting, and by the time the day was done, I hadn't accomplished anything I needed to get done. Why? Because I spent the day responding to what everyone else needed, my boss, my team, a new project, and someone asking for help. I was doing a lot... but I wasn't leading my day; it was leading me. Eventually, I decided to attend a leadership conference. That's when I heard John Maxwell speak live for the first time. He said something that stopped me in my tracks: "You have to set the intention for your day." Then he asked the room, "Do you know why?" His answer: "Because if you don't set the intention for your day, someone else will." He added, "Make sure you decide what you want to try to accomplish or what you want your day to look like because otherwise, you'll have a busy but unproductive life." I was tired of being busy. I wanted to be efficient. That moment shifted everything for me. Now, before I scroll, answer, or react, I pause. I set the tone with intention. Some days, it sounds like: "Today I will ensure my spouse knows she is loved." "Today, I will ensure my kids feel supported." "Today I'll communicate with clarity and confidence." Because if I don't lead my day, my day will lead me. Setting intention isn't about having the perfect plan; it's about knowing who and how you want to show up. It's not about perfection. It's about direction. And when I lead my day with clarity, I show up with more power, more peace, and more purpose. Don't just react to your day, lead it. The Best DISC Alignment S-type personality.

Action Steps:

Daily Action: Begin each morning by setting one clear intention for the day, whether it's to complete a specific task, practice patience, or stay focused on a goal.

Weekly Action: At the end of each week, review how setting daily intentions impacted your mindset and productivity. Adjust your intentions based on your priorities for the upcoming week.

"A gentle answer turns away wrath, but a harsh word

stirs up anger." Proverbs 15:1

Reacting is about emotion. Responding is about alignment. One protects the ego. The other protects the legacy. There was a time in my leadership journey when I believed being quick to act meant I was in control. If something went wrong, I addressed it. If something felt off, I spoke it. I didn't wait, I reacted. However, I started realizing something... Reacting isn't always leading. Sometimes, it's just emotion moving faster than wisdom. I remember one moment in particular that tested me deeply. Over the years, I have helped five different individuals put on events, behind the scenes. No credit needed. I didn't serve them for recognition; I did it because I believed in them. A few years later, an opportunity came up for a role I was selected for based on my passion, my leadership, and my ability to galvanize people. But suddenly, I was challenged by someone who asked: "What experience do you have?" That person had told everyone they didn't want the position... but clearly, they did. In that moment, I felt my emotions rise. I wanted to respond defensively. But I paused. Because that's the difference between reacting and responding. Reacting would've been about ego. Responding was about staying aligned. I reminded myself: I know my value. I know what I bring. I don't have to prove anything. I don't have to match energy that's misaligned with my character. That moment reminded me that responding is power under control. It's not about silence, it's about wisdom. It's about choosing clarity over chaos. It's about leading yourself before you lead others. Reacting is emotional. Responding is intentional. And leaders are called to be intentional. The Best DISC Alignment I-type personality.

Action Steps:

Daily Action: Whenever a challenge arises, take a deep breath before you respond. Ask yourself, "What outcome do I want here?" and choose your response accordingly.

Weekly Action: Reflect on any moments during the week where you reacted instead of responding. What could you have done differently? Practice this awareness to improve your future responses.

Step 4: Create a Personal Accountability System

"Commit your actions to the Lord, and your plans will succeed." Proverbs 16:3

Let's be honest, it's easy to talk about goals. It's even easier to get started on them. The hard part? Finishing without needing someone else to push you every step of the way. About six months before I retired from the military, I had a moment of realization: I need a system. For years, I was used to either giving directions or following them. Mission briefs. Orders. Objectives.

Feedback. The key ingredient behind all of that? It was always tied to a mission. The mission gave the structure meaning. And structure gave me discipline. So when that structure was about to be gone... I asked myself, "What's going to keep me aligned when the uniform comes off? "That's when I made the decision to create what I now call my personal accountability rhythm. Because here's the truth: If I always need someone else to hold me accountable... I haven't taken full ownership of my own vision. So I built a system not for show, not for social media, but for me. I started asking: "How do I hold myself accountable for the things that matter most?" "What will I track weekly to measure progress, not just busyness?" "How will I know if I'm living aligned — or just staying active?" And then I committed to a rhythm: Weekly review of my goals and habits. Visual dashboard of priorities. Check-ins with a mentor or trusted peer. Time-blocking for what really matters. Reflection without excuses is just correction and clarity. This isn't about pressure; it's about ownership. This is how I make sure I stay grounded in what matters, even when motivation fades. Because the version of me I'm becoming is the husband, father, leader, and builder I'm called to be, he doesn't get built off convenience. He gets built through rhythm, structure, and intention. Don't wait for pressure. Build your own system. The Best DISC Alignment D-type personality.

Action Steps:

Daily Action: At the end of each day, write down one action you took that aligned with your goals. Celebrate this as a win, no matter how small.

Weekly Action: Set aside time each week to review your progress, celebrate your wins, and identify areas for improvement. If possible, share your goals and progress with a trusted friend or mentor who can support your journey.

Reflection Prompts

Here are a few prompts to help you assess and strengthen

your proactive mindset:

What's one area of your life where you tend to react

rather than respond? How can you shift this?

What is one intention you could set each morning to keep

you focused and in control of your actions?

Who in your life can help keep you accountable for your

goals, and how can they support you?

Story of Transformation:

Deonte's Journey from Reactive to Proactive

My son, Deonte, has always had a passion for basketball. As he entered college and joined the basketball team, he quickly realized that the transition required more than just physical skill; it demanded mental resilience and a proactive mindset. In the early days, Deonte often found himself reacting to the intensity of college-level competition and the pressure of balancing academics with a rigorous athletic schedule.

Determined to succeed, Deonte decided to make a shift. He began each day with a specific intention, whether it was refining a particular skill, focusing on his studies, or practicing mindfulness to stay calm under pressure. He stopped reacting to setbacks and started approaching each challenge as an opportunity to grow. Instead of getting discouraged by a missed shot or a tough game, he used each experience as a lesson, making adjustments and staying focused on his long-term goals.

With this proactive approach, Deonte has not only become a stronger player but a resilient individual who's able to take control of his journey. His dedication serves as a reminder that no matter how challenging a situation may seem, we have the power to shape our response and take intentional steps forward.

Deonte's story demonstrates that the power shift from reactive to proactive can transform how we handle challenges, whether on the court or in life. When you decide to take control, focus on what you can improve, and approach each day with purpose, you create a foundation for success.

Bringing It All Together:

Building a Proactive Mindset

The power shift from reactive to proactive isn't something you achieve overnight; it's a practice. Each time you focus on what you can control, set intentions, and respond thoughtfully, you're building a foundation for resilience and success. By embracing this mindset, you'll find yourself better prepared to face challenges and more empowered to shape the life you envision.

Moving from reactive to proactive begins with small, intentional steps each day.

What three areas of your life would benefit from a proactive approach?

_____

_____

_____

What three daily intentions can you set to take control of your actions?

_____

_____

_____

What three strategies can help you respond thoughtfully instead of reacting impulsively?

_____

_____

_____

Final Reflection:

Empowering Yourself Through the Power Shift

When you choose to live proactively, you're taking responsibility for your future. Every day, you have the power to make choices that align with your goals and values. Embrace this shift, and let it transform how you approach each day. Remember, the power to shape your life lies in your hands, one intentional choice at a time.

CHAPTER 7: BUILDING RESILIENCE

"Consider it pure joy, my brothers and sisters, whenever you face trials of many kinds, because you know that the testing of your faith produces perseverance. Let perseverance finish its work so that you may be mature and complete, not lacking anything." James 1:2–4

Introduction:

The Power of Resilience Through Reflection

Resilience is often thought of as the ability to keep going despite challenges, but there's a secret ingredient that many people overlook: reflection. By taking time to reflect on experiences, both successes and setbacks, you give yourself the opportunity to learn, grow, and reinforce the strength you need to face future challenges. Reflection allows you to acknowledge your progress, understand what worked, and, perhaps most importantly, what didn't.

As philosopher Søren Kierkegaard said, "Life can only be understood backwards, but it must be lived forwards." This chapter is about looking back with purpose, learning from each step, and using those lessons to move forward with resilience.

My Journey: Finding Strength in Looking Back

Throughout my journey, I've encountered many challenges, and I realized early on that if I didn't take time to learn from each experience, I was bound to repeat the same mistakes. Reflecting on my experiences allowed me to process emotions, find clarity, and see each setback as a stepping stone rather than a roadblock.

Reflection became a powerful tool for building resilience in my life. It helped me recognize the growth that came from each challenge and appreciate the lessons that might have otherwise gone unnoticed. By making reflection a regular practice, I was able to develop a deeper sense of purpose and stay connected to my goals, even during tough times.

Reflection isn't just about thinking back on what happened; it's about intentional learning and growth. By making reflection a habit, you can build resilience and keep yourself grounded in what truly matters. This practice encourages mindfulness, keeps you focused on your progress, and helps you stay motivated even when the path gets tough.

Step 1: The Practice of Daily Reflection

"Examine yourselves to see whether you are in the faith; test yourselves." 2 Corinthians 13:5

Daily reflection is a simple but powerful way to end each day with purpose. This practice helps you process your experiences and prepares you to approach the next day with a fresh perspective.

For a long time, I didn't consider reflection a necessary habit. I wasn't a reader, and I thought I was too busy to slow down. But a mentor once told me, *"You don't grow just because time passes. You grow because you reflect."* That challenged me. One night, after a heavy day, I picked up *Funny How Life Works,* a book he recommended. I didn't expect much, but as I read, something clicked. I realized I'd been taking life too seriously and carrying pressure that wasn't mine to hold.

That night, I started a new habit: five quiet minutes before bed, asking myself three simple questions: what went well, what felt off, and what can I learn or let go of? That small practice changed everything. It brought peace, clarity, and reset my mindset. I began noticing what filled me and what drained me. I stopped carrying yesterday's weight into tomorrow. Reflection became a nightly reset, simple, powerful, and necessary. The Best DISC Alignment C-type personality.

Action Steps:

Daily Action: Each evening, spend a few minutes reflecting on your day. Ask yourself: "What went well today?" "What could I have done differently?" Write your answers to track growth over time.

Weekly Action: At the end of the week, review your reflections to spot patterns or lessons. Use these insights to adjust your mindset and approach.

Step 2: Celebrate Progress, No Matter How Small

"This is the day the Lord has made; we will rejoice and be

glad in it." Psalm 118:24

Resilience isn't just built by overcoming big challenges; it's also strengthened by recognizing small victories. Celebrating progress, even small steps, reinforces your sense of achievement and keeps you motivated to continue.

Honestly, there was a time I didn't celebrate anything unless it was huge. Helping someone get promoted didn't count it wasn't "my" win. Watching an entrepreneur I coached build a multimillion-dollar business? Great, but I was already chasing the next goal. Even when my daughter was excelling in volleyball or my marriage was thriving, I'd breeze right past those moments, always looking for something bigger.

But it hit me one day: I had been so focused on "more" that I overlooked what I already had: my beautiful wife, my growing kids, a home filled with love, a life I once prayed for. I had ignored the good stuff because it felt "too small" to celebrate. Now, I do it differently. I write down small wins. I pause and smile when I see my kids thriving. I thank God when my wife and I navigate a tough day. Those little things? They're not little at all; they're everything. The Best DISC Alignment I-type personality.

Action Steps:

Daily Action: Celebrate one small success each day, completing a task, staying patient, or encouraging someone.

Weekly Action: Reflect on these moments and how they're adding up. Acknowledge the beauty of progress in motion.

"And we know that in all things God works for the good of those who love him, who have been called according to his purpose." Romans 8:28

Reflection is especially important when it comes to setbacks. By taking time to analyze what went wrong and why, you can turn challenges into valuable learning experiences that strengthen your resilience.

There was a time when I got in trouble for doing what I loved: coaching, speaking, and putting on events. One event was a huge success, and I thought I was stepping into my purpose. But shortly after, people questioned my intentions. There were misunderstandings about how I was balancing my full-time job with what I was building outside of it.

It caught me off guard, and honestly, it hurt. But that moment taught me a lot. I learned about the importance of planning, communication, and protecting your vision. It was a painful experience, but it shaped me. I learned that not everyone who supports you publicly is rooting for you privately. Still, I chose to lead better, speak clearly, and keep helping people thrive. That setback didn't stop me; it sharpened me. The Best DISC Alignment D-type personality.

Action Steps:

Daily Action: When you face a setback, reflect. Ask, "What did I learn from this?" and write it down.

Weekly Action: Review your setbacks. Use them as teaching tools to strengthen your future decisions.

Step 4: Revisit Your Purpose and Goals Regularly

"Let your eyes look straight ahead; fix your gaze directly before you." Proverbs 4:25

Reflection is also a time to reconnect with your larger purpose and goals. By revisiting your "why," you remind yourself of what truly matters, which can be a powerful motivator during tough times.

Recently, my wife, Sharita, and I were talking about how packed my schedule was, speaking, coaching, volunteering, and she said, *"You can't keep doing things that aren't aligned with your purpose."* She wasn't being critical. She was right. I had let good intentions become distractions.

So I got back to my foundation: Why am I doing this? To help business owners grow. To build thriving teams. To raise the standard of customer service. That clarity grounded me. It reminded me that purpose isn't just a feel-good phrase; it's a boundary. It's how I protect my energy and focus. Now, I run everything through that filter. If it's not aligned, it's not for me. The Best DISC Alignment S-type personality.

Action Steps:

Daily Action: Start each morning with a short reminder of your "why."

Weekly Action: Reflect on how your time and choices aligned with your purpose. Make adjustments if needed.

Reflection Prompts

Use these prompts to start your habit of daily and weekly reflection:

What's one lesson from this week that you want to carry forward?

What small progress did you make today that deserves celebration?

How has a recent setback helped you grow or clarify your path?

Story of Transformation:

Jordan Finding Purpose through Mentorship

During my time working in a clinic, I met Jordan, an optometry apprentice who was part of a military internship program. At first, he struggled to find purpose in his role. Though he was committed, he often questioned whether optometry was the right path and felt uncertain about his future. His work felt routine, and he couldn't always see the impact he was making.

Then, he connected with a mentor through the internship program, a seasoned optometrist who had also served in the military. This mentor introduced him to the power of reflection and encouraged him to treat each day as a learning opportunity. After clinic hours, they would sit down and talk, reflecting on the day's challenges, identifying small wins, and celebrating the positive outcomes in patients' lives.

Through this process, Jordan began to see his work differently. Each patient interaction held more meaning. He realized he wasn't just checking boxes; he was building trust, creating impact, and growing in his purpose. Reflection gave Jordan confidence, and mentorship helped him believe in the contribution he was making. Over time, he transformed from someone unsure of his direction into a professional with clarity, purpose, and resilience.

Jordan's story is a reminder that reflection is more than a quiet habit; it's a powerful shift in mindset. And sometimes, all it takes is the right perspective and the right person to help you see what's already inside you.

Bringing It All Together: The Habit of Reflection

Building resilience isn't about avoiding challenges; it's about learning from them. By making reflection a regular habit, you give yourself the gift of clarity, peace, and purpose. You learn from your wins and your wounds. You grow stronger from stillness. And you develop the kind of resilience that can't be shaken by external storms because it's anchored within.

What three questions can you ask yourself daily to reflect

on your experiences?

_____

_____

_____

What three small wins can you look for each day to

celebrate progress?

_____

_____

_____

What three goals or purposes will you revisit regularly to

stay focused on your journey?

_____

_____

_____

Final Reflection:

Strengthening Resilience through Looking Back

When you make time to reflect, you're not just looking back; you're building the resilience to move forward with purpose. Each lesson, each small win, and each setback you process strengthens you for the path ahead. Embrace reflection as a tool for growth, and let it empower you to become the best version of yourself, resilient and ready for whatever comes next.

CHAPTER 8: PRACTICING PATIENCE

"Let us not become weary in doing good, for at the proper time we will reap a harvest if we do not give up."

Galatians 6:9

Introduction: The Power Of Patience

In a world that celebrates instant gratification, patience often feels like a forgotten virtue. Yet, success isn't built overnight; it's the result of consistent effort, small victories, and a steadfast commitment to long-term goals. Patience is the bridge between where you are and where you want to be. As Aristotle said, "Patience is bitter, but its fruit is sweet." This chapter explores how cultivating patience can transform your journey, allowing you to embrace progress and find joy in the process.

My Journey: Writing this Book

Patience hasn't always been my strength, and writing this book has been one of the most profound lessons in waiting with purpose. There were countless moments when I felt stuck when the words didn't flow, the ideas felt scattered, and the end seemed far out of reach.

But I knew this book was more than just a personal goal; it was a message meant to inspire others. I learned to celebrate small victories, like finishing a chapter or finding just the right story to include. I reminded myself of the purpose behind these pages, knowing that every delay and revision was sharpening and shaping something meaningful.

Through this process, I discovered that patience isn't about sitting still; it's about persevering with intention. Writing this book taught me to trust the journey and embrace the growth that comes from persistence. This shift in mindset transformed what once felt overwhelming into a labor of love and purpose.

The Pillars of Practicing Patience

Patience is the quiet strength that keeps you grounded. It's the understanding that meaningful change doesn't happen overnight and that true progress requires steady, intentional effort. When you practice patience, you build the resilience to keep going, even when results aren't immediate, and you learn to find joy in the journey itself.

Step 1: Setting Long-Term and Short-Term Goals

"Write the vision and make it plain... Though it tarries, wait for it; because it will surely come, it will not delay."

Habakkuk 2:2-3

Patience becomes easier when you recognize the progress you're making along the way. Celebrating small wins helps you stay motivated and reminds you that *every step counts.* One story that captures this perfectly is my friend and business partner, Dr. Ben Thayil.

Dr. Ben is a seasoned optometrist out of Miami who built a thriving private practice, but like so many high-performing professionals, he reached a point where success on the outside didn't feel like success on the inside. Behind the scenes, he was overwhelmed. He was wearing every hat: doctor, owner, leader, fixer, and it was draining him. Year after year, he quietly asked himself if it was time to sell the practice and walk away.

But instead of giving up, Dr. Ben made a decision. He stopped chasing *more* and started building with *intention*. That one shift changed everything. He carved out time to reflect; he got honest about what was working and what wasn't. Then he set new goals, not just for the business, but for himself as a leader, a husband, a dad, and a man. He began leaning into what he calls the "invisible curriculum," the soft skills no one teaches: communication, boundaries, leadership, team culture, and vision.

As he added structure, his clarity grew. His team grew. And that quiet feeling of burnout? It started to lift.

Dr. Ben didn't just write down long-term goals; he paired them with short-term, intentional steps that gave him traction. He stopped trying to do it all alone and started building systems that allowed *everyone* to win.

That same practice that once felt like a burden became a mission. And now, he's using that journey to help others, teaching providers how to lead with purpose, build healthy teams, and rekindle the joy in their work.

Dr. Ben's story reminds us that you don't fix burnout with busyness, you fix it with belief, structure, and small, consistent wins that build long-term resilience.

Because when you combine vision with discipline, and give yourself room to reflect, you don't just wait for things to change… You start *becoming* the change. That's the power of setting goals with patience. Not just writing them down, but walking them out, one step at a time. The Best DISC Alignment C-type personality.

Action Steps:

Daily Action: At the end of each day, write down one small achievement you're proud of.

Weekly Action: Reflect on how these small wins contribute to your larger goals. Share them with a friend or mentor for encouragement.

Step 2: Shift Your Perspective

"Do not conform to the pattern of this world, but be transformed by the renewing of your mind." Romans 12:2

Patience is not about passivity; it's about actively trusting the process. By shifting your focus from the destination to the journey, you'll find greater fulfillment in the present moment.

There was a point in my life when I measured everything by one thing: income. Title? Cool. Position? Respected. Paycheck? Steady. But fulfillment? It was missing. I was showing up, but I wasn't being pulled by purpose.

That's when I made a shift. I stopped asking, *"How much can I make?"* and started asking, *"How much impact can I create?"* It wasn't easy. Letting go of the familiar to chase something more meaningful is uncomfortable. But I didn't want to spend my life climbing ladders; I wanted to build ladders for others.

Today, I live with a different perspective. I focus on adding value, growing leaders, and helping others shift culture through their leadership. The income still comes, but the fulfillment fuels me. If you're feeling stuck, maybe it's not your effort; it's your perspective. Shift from chasing money to creating meaning, and watch everything begin to align.

The Best DISC Alignment I-type personality.

Action Steps:

Daily Action: Practice mindfulness by focusing on one task at a time, fully immersing yourself in the experience.

Weekly Action: Identify a moment during the week when you felt impatient. Reflect on how you can reframe that experience to see the growth it offered.

Step 3: Honor the Season You're In

"There is a time for everything, and a season for every

activity under the heavens." Ecclesiastes 3:1

When you're committed to long-term success, it's easy to feel frustrated in seasons where the results aren't immediate. But growth doesn't always look like forward motion; sometimes it looks like staying planted, learning, and becoming stronger from the inside out.

I remember a time when I felt stuck. I had built the systems, created the content, and laid the foundation, but I kept holding back. I wanted everything to be perfect before launching. I was tweaking, delaying, and quietly comparing myself to others.

Then Sharita looked at me and said something that stopped me: *"You're already ready. The only person keeping score is you."* That hit hard. I was measuring myself by pressure. But the truth was, I wasn't behind. I was in a preparation season.

So I stopped fighting the season and started honoring it. I let go of perfection and chose to be faithful instead. From that space came deeper clarity, stronger systems, and renewed peace.

If you're in a season that feels slow or unclear, pause. The delay might not be denial; it might be development. Honor the season. The Best DISC Alignment S-type personality.

Action Steps:

Daily Action: Ask yourself, "What is this season teaching me?" Write it down or reflect on it during quiet time.

Weekly Action: Identify one area where you've been fighting the season instead of flowing with it. Shift your focus to faithfulness over frustration.

Step 4: Trust the Timing

"But those who hope in the Lord will renew their strength... They will run and not grow weary; they will walk and not be faint." Isaiah 40:31

Sometimes, the results we seek require time to unfold. Trusting the timing of your journey means letting go of the need for control and embracing faith in the process.

Publishing this book taught me that lesson in a powerful way. There were countless moments I felt stuck when the words wouldn't come, when the message didn't feel clear, when the finish line kept moving. I originally wrote the draft in 2019, and I'll admit that at first, I just wanted to publish it so I could say I did.

But something shifted. I remembered what I tell my kids all the time: *"The way you do one thing is the way you do everything."* That made me pause. I didn't want this to just be a finished product; I wanted it to reflect legacy. I started showing up with intention. I celebrated small wins: a finished paragraph, a clear chapter, a title that finally clicked. The delays weren't wasted; they were shaping something better. Patience taught me to trust the unseen growth. In a world of instant gratification, I chose the long view.

If you're in a slow season, don't quit. Don't compare. Trust the timing. God is still working, even when it feels quiet. The Best DISC Alignment D-type personality.

Action Steps:

Daily Action: When you feel impatient, take a deep breath and remind yourself that growth takes time.

Weekly Action: Reflect on a time when patience led to a positive outcome. Use that experience as a reminder to trust the timing of your current goals.

Reflection Prompts

Use these prompts to explore how patience plays a role in your journey:

What's one area of your life where you've struggled with impatience? How can you reframe that experience?

How have small wins contributed to your larger goals?

What's one step you can take this week to stay connected to your purpose?

Story of Transformation:

Jamie's Journey to Success through Patience

My friend Jamie has always been entrepreneurial, even during her years in the mental health field. She wasn't just committed to helping her clients heal; she was constantly looking for ways to make things better, both for others and herself.

That mindset carried over when she decided to pivot from mental health into building her own business, one centered around personal development, conflict management, and team building. It was a big leap, but Jamie was no stranger to transformation.

In the early stages, when she transitioned from mental health private practice management, she faced what many new entrepreneurs face: inconsistency. Clients were coming in, but the income was unpredictable. Some days felt full of momentum, while others felt like waiting rooms for progress. But instead of letting discouragement win, Jamie got focused.

She set short-term goals: land her first five clients, tighten up her message, and show up consistently. At the same time, she kept her eyes on the long-term vision: building a business that created real impact and sustainability over time, and then came the shift.

Jamie realized that working only with individuals wasn't going to get her where she wanted to go. Rather than panic or push harder, she took a step back and *shifted her perspective*. She recognized that her strength wasn't just in one-on-one sessions, but in equipping teams and organizations with tools for emotional resilience and leadership. So, she transitioned her model. She honored the season she was in, one that required structure, scalability, and bold moves. She rebranded, restructured, and began offering B2B services that opened doors to larger contracts and more consistent revenue. It didn't happen overnight. But it happened *because* she was patient, intentional, and anchored in purpose.

Jamie's story is a reminder that patience isn't about waiting; it's about *working wisely* while you wait. It's setting clear goals, embracing new seasons, and trusting that every pivot can serve your purpose. She didn't just survive the transition; she stepped into her next level. Now, she's not only leading from experience, she's building something that empowers others to do the same.

Bringing It All Together:

Cultivating Patience for Long-Term Success

Patience is not about waiting passively; it's about staying committed, celebrating progress, and trusting the process. By practicing patience, you create space for growth, resilience, and success. Remember, the journey is just as important as the destination.

Write down three small wins from this week and how they've moved you closer to your goal.

_____

_____

_____

What three actions can you take to stay connected to your "why"?

_____

_____

_____

Write a short statement about your "why" and place it somewhere you'll see it daily.

_____

_____

_____

Final Reflection: Embrace the Journey

Success is rarely immediate, but it's always worth the wait. By practicing patience, you allow yourself to grow, learn, and thrive in ways you never imagined. Trust the timing of your journey and remember that every small step forward is a victory. The sweet fruit of patience awaits those who persevere.

"Let your eyes look straight ahead; fix your gaze directly

before you. Give careful thought to the paths for your

feet... do not turn to the right or the left."

Proverbs 4:25–27

Introduction: The Power of Focus

In a world filled with constant notifications, multitasking, and endless to-do lists, maintaining focus has become a rare but essential skill. True progress toward any goal requires sustained attention and the ability to stay engaged, even when distractions are everywhere. Focus isn't just about eliminating distractions; it's about learning to prioritize what matters most and dedicating time to deep, intentional work.

As Steve Jobs famously said, *"Focus is about saying no."* This chapter is about cultivating the discipline to say no to what doesn't serve your goals, so you can fully commit to what does.

Finding Focus Despite Many Commitments

Maintaining focus hasn't always been easy for me. Balancing multiple responsibilities, family, career, personal goals, and even writing this book has often felt like being pulled in a dozen directions at once. At times, I'd find myself trying to do everything at once, only to realize that nothing was getting the attention it deserved. To truly make progress, I knew I had to find a way to prioritize and focus on one task at a time. I began implementing small changes, like setting specific times for each task, reducing distractions, and practicing single-tasking. These shifts helped me concentrate on what mattered most, and each step forward felt more intentional and impactful. Learning to focus taught me that sometimes, doing less is actually doing more.

Mastering focus means creating boundaries that protect your time and energy. It's about saying no to distractions so you can say yes to your goals. When you prioritize deep, focused work, you make meaningful progress and build the discipline to stay committed even when distractions try to pull you away.

Step 1: Eliminate Distractions

"Let us throw off everything that hinders and the sin that so easily entangles. And let us run with perseverance the race marked out for us." Hebrews 12:1

Distractions are everywhere, and while it's impossible to eliminate them completely, you can create an environment that minimizes their impact.

There was a moment I'll never forget. Everyone else was relaxing, hanging out, just enjoying the evening, and I was locked in, working on my presentation. I had invited a few close friends over, but not to kick back. We spent hours refining our presentations, tightening our delivery, and giving each other honest feedback. While others coasted, we were preparing.

The next day at the event, the difference showed. Most presenters looked tired and scattered. But the three of us? We were energized, clear, and we nailed it. That night reminded me of something I live by: *"If you want the same results as everyone else, do what they're doing. But if you want something different, you've got to show up differently."*

Distractions aren't always obvious; they sneak in through good times, well-meaning people, and comfortable routines. But focus? That's intentional. It takes discipline. And when your moment comes, you won't rise to the occasion; you'll rise to the level of your preparation. The best DISC Alignment D-type personality.

Action Steps:

Daily Action: Identify one common distraction (like checking your phone) and commit to reducing its impact. Set your phone aside, turn off notifications, or create a distraction-free workspace.

Weekly Action: Reflect on your progress. What strategies helped? What can be improved?

Step 2: Practice Single-Tasking

"There is a time for everything, and a season for every activity under the heavens." Ecclesiastes 3:1

Multitasking can feel productive, but it often leads to missed details and mental burnout. Single-tasking, giving your full attention to one thing at a time, brings clarity, peace, and excellence.

I learned this the hard way while working as a Chief Experience Officer. One of my key responsibilities was to send promotional communication drafts directly to the hospital director. But one week, I started getting feedback that didn't match what I had designed. It felt off. I started second-guessing myself. Was I slipping? Was I too tired? Did I miss something?

Eventually, I discovered the issue. My former director, who hadn't been updated on the new workflow, was still reviewing and editing my drafts before passing them along. It wasn't intentional sabotage, just a lack of communication. But the moment that really stuck with me wasn't the mix-up; it was the fact that I hadn't caught it sooner. I had been too distracted to notice the red flags. That's when it hit me: I wasn't failing because I was incapable. I was failing because I was fragmented. I had been trying to do everything, managing multiple deadlines, coaching sessions, and side projects all at once. My mind was everywhere, and as a result, I wasn't fully present anywhere.

That moment became a turning point. I realized that focus isn't just a skill; it's protection. It protects your peace, your clarity, and your confidence. When you're fully locked in, you don't just do better work, you feel more grounded. You spot issues faster, make decisions with more clarity, and regain your edge.

If you've been feeling off, scattered, or stretched thin, maybe it's not because you're doing too little, but because you're doing too much all at once. Sometimes the most powerful move isn't pushing harder; it's slowing down and giving one thing your full attention.

The best DISC Alignment C-type personality.

Action Steps:

Daily Action: Choose one task to focus on for a set period. Don't switch until it's complete.

Weekly Action: Reflect on your experience. What improved when you gave your full attention to one thing?

Step 3: Set Boundaries Around Your Time

"Be very careful, then, how you live not as unwise but as

wise, making the most of every opportunity..."

Ephesians 5: 15-16

Time boundaries help you protect your focus and energy. There was a season where I said yes to everything that called, opportunities, favors. Not because I didn't value my time, but because I genuinely wanted to help. But I started to realize: every yes is also a no. When I said yes to every request, I was unintentionally saying no to my goals, my health, and my creativity.

My priorities took the hit. I kept pushing back projects that mattered to me. Eventually, I had to draw a line. I started protecting blocks of time not to isolate myself, but to create something meaningful. Helping others win doesn't mean you have to lose in the process.

Now, I guard my time not just for productivity, but for significance. Because people aren't just watching what you do, they're watching how you lead, how you rest, how you protect what matters most. If you're constantly saying yes and wondering why you feel scattered, check your boundaries. You weren't made to carry everything, just what aligns with your assignment. The best DISC Alignment S-type personality.

Action Steps:

Daily Action: Block time for what matters. Communicate that boundary clearly.

Weekly Action: Evaluate how well you honored that boundary. What can you adjust?

Step 4: Prioritize Deep Work

"Whatever you do, work at it with all your heart, as working for the Lord, not for human masters."

Colossians 3:23

Deep work is focused time for high-impact tasks. It's the space where your best ideas and clearest breakthroughs happen. There was a day I was preparing for a keynote. I was locked in studying, refining, and praying over my message. That's when a friend messaged me, asking for "a quick coaching session." And then a business partner asked if I could jump in on a deal. Normally, I would've said yes without blinking.

But that day, I paused. I responded to both with a kind but clear no. Not because I didn't care, but because I was already committed to my message, my moment, my purpose. That decision changed everything. We delivered a powerful keynote, and the team handled the other things just fine.

That moment taught me this: Saying no to the urgent protects your ability to show up for the important. Deep work isn't selfish; it's strategic. It multiplies your impact. It allows you to lead with clarity and serve with excellence. If you feel stretched thin, trying to do everything for everyone, take a breath. You're not failing, you're just due for a focus reset. The best DISC Alignment I-type personality.

Action Steps:

Daily Action: Schedule one focused work session each day with zero interruptions.

Weekly Action: Review what came from those sessions. Were you more effective? What tasks benefited most?

What distractions most often pull your attention away from your goals? How can you minimize their impact?

When have you experienced the benefits of single-tasking? What made it effective?

How can setting time boundaries help you focus on what matters most?

What tasks in your life would benefit from dedicated deep work sessions?

Story of Transformation:

Jaylen's Journey to Focus

My middle son, Jaylen, is a college athlete balancing early morning workouts, late-night assignments, young men's shenanigans, and everything in between. Between practices, classes, personal goals, and the pressure to perform in all of them, it was a lot. Like many students, he started off trying to juggle everything at once. He wanted to show up strong in every area, but the result was the opposite: he was overwhelmed, stretched thin, and constantly chasing the next thing without fully being present. It felt like he had too many demands, too many voices, and too many open tabs in his mind.

Eventually, Jaylen made a choice. He didn't wait for the schedule to slow down or the pressure to ease up. He focused. He started practicing single-tasking, mastering one basketball move at a time, finishing assignments with full attention, and learning to be fully present wherever his feet were. He set boundaries around his time, eliminated distractions, and carved out time for deep work. Whether that meant putting his phone away during study hours or saying no to hangouts that didn't align with his goals, he began guarding his energy. The shift wasn't just academic or athletic; it was internal. His performance sharpened. His grades improved. But more than anything, his focus gave birth to clarity, and that clarity gave him confidence.

Recently, Jaylen heard me speak live for the first time. I shared one of my favorite declarations with the audience: "I am _____, and that's the way I want it to be." I also challenged them to define their own version of success and wealth, not what others expect, but what aligns with who they are. That message hit home for Jaylen. Afterward, he told me, "That part about success and wealth... I never thought of it like that. And when you said, 'I am _____, and that's the way I want it to be,' I'm taking it further. I now say, 'I am _____, and that's the way I want it to be because that's who I am and how it is.'" That wasn't just a moment of reflection; it was a moment of identity.

And with that identity came a decision. Jaylen chose to join the United States Air Force. Not because he was unsure, but because he was finally clear. He's not chasing every opportunity; he's owning his next step with purpose. His journey reminds me that focus isn't just about doing more. It's about doing what matters most with clarity, consistency, and purpose. Because when you eliminate distractions and narrow your energy, you multiply your impact. And when you own your identity, you shape your future on your terms.

Bringing It All Together: The Discipline of Focus

Mastering focus is about discipline and intentionality. It's about choosing to prioritize your goals over distractions, creating a workspace that fosters concentration, and dedicating time to meaningful work. With focus, you gain clarity, make consistent progress, and develop the resilience to pursue your dreams in a world full of noise.

What three distractions can you reduce or eliminate to create a more focused environment?

_____

_____

_____

What three tasks can you prioritize for single-tasking each day?

_____

_____

_____

What three time boundaries can you set to protect your deep work sessions?

_____

_____

_____

Focus is a skill that can transform how you approach your goals. By reducing distractions, practicing single-tasking, setting boundaries, and prioritizing deep work, you gain the clarity and discipline needed to achieve meaningful progress. Remember, focus is about choosing what matters most and committing fully to it. Embrace focus as a tool for success, and watch how it brings you closer to your dreams.

CHAPTER 10: CREATE ACCOUNTABILITY

"As iron sharpens iron, so one person sharpens another."

Proverbs 27:17

Introduction: The Power of Accountability

Accountability is often described as a partnership in progress. Having people in your life who encourage you, hold you accountable, and support you through challenges can be a game-changer. Accountability isn't just about achieving goals faster; it's about building resilience, learning from feedback, and having the strength to keep going when the path gets tough. When you invite accountability into your life, you create a foundation of support that makes success more attainable and the journey more meaningful.

As Helen Keller said, "Alone we can do so little; together we can do so much." This chapter is about finding strength in accountability, creating connections that keep you focused, and building a support system that helps you achieve your dreams.

My Journey To Building Accountability Networks

Throughout my journey, accountability has been essential to staying on track with my goals, from personal aspirations to professional ambitions. There were times when I thought I could do it all on my own, but I quickly learned the value of having people who were invested in my success. Accountability partners, mentors, and supportive friends became my sounding boards, guiding me through challenges and reminding me of my purpose.

One of the most powerful examples of accountability in my life has been in writing this book. The process required more than just personal dedication; it took a network of support to stay focused and push through the tougher moments. My accountability partners encouraged me to keep going, provided honest feedback, and celebrated each milestone with me. Having people who believed in me made all the difference, and I learned that accountability is more than just sharing goals; it's about creating lasting connections that lift you up and keep you grounded.

The Pillars of Accountability:

Accountability isn't about control; it's about commitment. It's about aligning your actions with your values, surrounding yourself with people who support your growth, and taking intentional steps toward your goals. True accountability isn't just external; it's also internal. It requires honesty, discipline, and the willingness to acknowledge both progress and setbacks.

By embracing accountability, you create a culture of continuous improvement, one where challenges become learning opportunities, milestones become celebrations, and progress becomes a shared journey. Whether through trusted partners, public commitments, or self-reflection, accountability strengthens your resilience and keeps you moving forward.

As you continue this journey, ask yourself: Who in my life can help me stay accountable? What commitments will keep me on track? And most importantly, how will I use accountability as a tool for growth?

Step 1: Find an Accountability Partner

"Two are better than one... If either of them falls down, one can help the other up." Ecclesiastes 4:9–10

A few years ago, while I was stationed in Japan, I sat down with a trusted advisor, someone I deeply respected. During our conversation, he walked me through what he called the "7 Ps," seven principles he believed were essential for building a strong, purposeful life. Every one of them hit home. But then he paused, looked me in the eye, and said something I'll never forget: *"Cristian, no matter how strong you are, you need an accountability partner, someone who will tell you the truth in love and always steer you in the right direction."* That conversation shifted my mindset.

Later, I sat down with Sharita and said, "We're going to do this for each other. We're going to hold each other accountable not just when it's easy, but when it's inconvenient and uncomfortable." Since then, I've intentionally asked several people to be that for me: mentors, leaders, and close friends. People I trust to challenge me, stretch me, and keep me grounded. And I've done the same for them. This one shift has paid off in so many ways. From publishing accredited articles to writing this book, from building businesses to staying consistent as a husband and father, accountability has been the difference between intention and follow-through. The best DISC Alignment S-type personality.

Action Steps:

Daily: Reach out to someone who can serve as your accountability partner.

Weekly: Check in with them to share wins, struggles, and next steps.

Step 2: Set Public Commitments

"Let your light shine before others, that they may see your good deeds and glorify your Father in heaven."

Matthew 5:16

A while back, I made a bold decision: I committed to going live every single day for an entire year. I hit "post" and within minutes got two messages. One from a friend: *"I'm holding you to it."* The other from someone even closer: *"Do you really want to commit to something that long?"* That second message, the doubt became fuel. I didn't want average results. I wanted something more. And that's exactly what public commitment created.

That single decision turned into over 500 straight days of showing up. No excuses. No shortcuts. I gained more than content; I gained clarity, consistency, and confidence. Going public with your goals might feel risky. But sometimes, that pressure is exactly what you need to activate the version of yourself that's been waiting to rise.

The best DISC Alignment D-type personality.

Action Steps:

Daily: Share one goal with a trusted group or publicly.

Weekly: Reflect on what helped or challenged your consistency and adjust.

Step 3: Regular Self-Check-Ins

"Let us examine our ways and test them, and let us return to the Lord." Lamentations 3:40

One night, I sat at my desk completely frustrated. I had been busy all day, but it didn't feel like I made any real progress. I wasn't lazy. I wasn't even distracted. But something felt *off*.

Then I remembered something I used to teach my customer service teams: Always keep a mirror by the phone. Before they answered a call, I'd ask them to check their energy. Were they smiling? Were they ready to serve? That night, it hit me that I wasn't doing that for myself. So I wrote a simple question on a sticky note: "Did I move closer to my purpose today?" From that moment on, I made it a habit to pause each evening and ask myself three things:

1. Did I stay aligned with my priorities?
2. What distracted me, and how can I fix it tomorrow?
3. What small win can I celebrate?

That 5-minute check-in became one of my most powerful tools. I call habits. I stopped making excuses. And I started noticing the small wins that were quietly building something big. The best DISC Alignment C-type personality.

Action Steps:

Daily: Ask yourself one focus question each evening.

Weekly: Block out 15 minutes to review where you are and what needs adjusting.

Step 4: Celebrate Milestones

With Accountability Partners

"Rejoice with those who rejoice; mourn with those who

mourn." Romans 12:15

We had just wrapped up a major training series with a brand-new client, a contract we had been preparing for over several months. The day went better than expected. We hit our marks, made a real impact, and received great feedback.

But the moment that stayed with me came after the event. I got a text from my accountability partner: *"You crushed your presentation. I saw all your preparation show up today. I'm proud of you. More to come."*

That message hit different. Not because of what was said but because of *who* said it. Someone who had been watching the journey, not just the outcome. Someone who had seen the long nights, the setbacks, the sacrifices. And that moment reminded me: it's not just about the finish line, it's about the people who walk with you to get there. The best DISC Alignment I-type personality.

Action Steps:

Daily: Acknowledge your small wins with someone who's walking with you.

Weekly: Celebrate milestones in a meaningful way, notes, check-ins, or time together.

Story of Transformation:

My Wife's Journey to Certification

Sharita, my wife, is a living example of what accountability can do. As a leader, mother, and future licensed marriage and family therapist, she had a lot on her plate, but she never let that become an excuse. She invited accountability early on, and we committed to being that for each other.

We planned together, checked in often, celebrated small wins, and made space for honest conversations. Whether she was preparing for an exam, tackling a tough assignment, or navigating her devotional, accountability gave her the structure and strength to keep going.

Today, she's thriving and using that same resilience to help others do the same.

Bringing It All Together:

The Power of Shared Goals

Accountability isn't just about results; it's about *relationships*. When you walk with others through public commitments, quiet check-ins, tough feedback, and shared wins, you build something that lasts. Don't try to do it alone. Find your team. Set your standards. Check in often. And celebrate every step.

Accelerate Your Success: Implementation Exercise

Accountability doesn't happen by accident; it happens through intention. This exercise is designed to help you take the insights from this chapter and *immediately* apply them in real life. Don't overthink it. Just start. Clarity will come as you move.

Who are three people who could be valuable

accountability partners on your journey?

_____

_____

_____

What three public commitments can you make this

week to help you stay focused on your goals? Think of

goals that matter.

_____

_____

_____

What three questions will you ask yourself during

weekly self-check-ins to stay aligned and focused?

_____

_____

_____

Final Reflection:

Embracing Accountability as a Path to Growth

Accountability is more than a strategy; it's a mindset. It's a decision not to walk alone. A decision to invite challenge, embrace feedback, and celebrate progress along the way. Whether it's through a single conversation, a late-night text, or a quiet moment of reflection in the mirror, accountability is what turns good intentions into real results.

And the truth is, the most successful people don't just have discipline. They have people. And those people make all the difference. Let this be the chapter where you stop trying to carry it all alone and start building the kind of accountability that lifts you higher and keeps you aligned with your purpose.

CHAPTER 11: OVERCOMING SELF-SABOTAGE

"We take captive every thought to make it obedient to

Christ." 2 Corinthians 10:5

Introduction: The Battle Within

For many of us, one of the biggest obstacles to success isn't external, it's internal. Self-sabotage can show up as procrastination, perfectionism, negative self-talk, or the fear of failure. These behaviors keep us from reaching our full potential, often holding us back in ways we don't even realize. Overcoming self-sabotage isn't easy, but when you recognize and address these patterns, you can take meaningful steps toward growth.

As author and psychologist Dr. Maxwell Maltz said, "We are our own worst critics, and sometimes, our own biggest enemies." This chapter is about understanding the roots of self-sabotage and equipping yourself with the tools to overcome it, so you can finally step out of your own way and embrace your potential.

My Journey:

Recognizing and Tackling My Own Patterns

Like many people, I've encountered moments of self-sabotage in my own journey. There were times when I would set ambitious goals but delay starting, unsure if I was capable of meeting them. Other times, I'd get caught up in perfecting details, so much so that it kept me from moving forward. Over time, I began to see that these patterns were rooted in self-doubt and fear of making mistakes.

To overcome these habits, I had to make a conscious choice to recognize my patterns and find strategies to counter them. I learned to start before I felt "ready," to embrace progress over perfection, and to quiet the doubts that tried to hold me back. This journey of tackling self-sabotage taught me that while overcoming these behaviors is a daily practice, each small victory brings you closer to reaching your goals.

Self-sabotage doesn't just happen; it follows a pattern. The good news? Patterns can be broken. These four pillars are key to disrupting that cycle and moving forward with clarity and purpose. When you learn to identify your triggers, challenge your beliefs, interrupt harmful habits, and redefine what success really looks like, you begin to take back control. These pillars don't just help you move faster... they help you move freer.

Step 1: Identify Your Triggers

"Search me, God, and know my heart... See if there is any offensive way in me, and lead me in the way everlasting."

Psalm 139 :23–24

I used to think self-sabotage was just about procrastination or discipline until I realized it was deeper than that. It was a battle within me. I'd get close to finishing something meaningful, and suddenly I'd feel tired, distracted, or unsure. It could be as simple as not wanting to work out, even though I had a goal in mind. I wasn't afraid of failing. I was afraid of what might happen if I *succeeded*. Would people think I changed? Could I really handle the pressure? Who might I lose in the process?

I delayed launching my book, even though I'd taught the content for years. Same with programs people asked me to create. I hesitated not because the content wasn't ready... but because deep down, I wasn't sure *I* was.

Everything started shifting when I slowed down and began identifying my triggers. For me, it happened when things felt "too easy," when visibility increased, or when people started expecting more. That's when I'd pull back from purpose. Once I recognized those moments, I stopped reacting and started fighting *for* my calling instead of against it. The best DISC Alignment C-type personality.

Action Steps:

Daily: Pause when you're avoiding a task and ask, "What am I really feeling right now?"

Weekly: Reflect on the moments you felt resistance and trace them back to the trigger.

Step 2: Challenge Limiting Beliefs

"Finally, brothers and sisters, whatever is true, whatever is noble, whatever is right... think about such things." —

Philippians 4:8

For years, I thought my biggest roadblock was time or strategy. But the real issue? It was the voice in my head whispering things like:

"Maybe you're not enough."

"Who do you think you are?"

"Don't speak too boldly."

"Money doesn't grow on trees."

These weren't just thoughts; they were beliefs I had picked up from my environment, upbringing, and even past disappointments. They didn't sound like fear; they sounded like logic. But they were lies disguised as realism.

It wasn't until I asked myself, *Who told me that?* that I started to see the truth. If that belief didn't come from God, why was I giving it so much power?

That's when I started replacing those lies with truth:

"I am capable."

"I am prepared."

"I am gifted."

"I am a champion."

"And that's the way I want it to be."

That last line came from a Bible study. My friend Monica said, "Whatever you say after 'I am,' follow it with 'and that's the way I want it to be.'" That simple shift made me more intentional with my words. It wasn't just a motivational trick; it became a declaration of direction. If you're stuck, maybe it's not your schedule or your strategy. Maybe it's the belief you've been rehearsing too long. You can change that today. The best DISC Alignment I-type personality.

Action Steps:

Daily: Write down one limiting belief and challenge it with truth.

Weekly: Choose one belief to replace and speak your new affirmation out loud every day.

Step 3: Interrupt the Pattern

"See, I am doing a new thing! Now it springs up; do you not perceive it?" Isaiah 43:19

There were seasons when I wasn't lazy; I was just stuck in a rut. I showed up, checked boxes, and kept moving... but something felt off. I wasn't stuck because I lacked vision. I was stuck because I hadn't taken time to *reset*. So I started interrupting the pattern.

When I caught myself scrolling, stalling, or endlessly tweaking, I made myself get up. Walk. Breathe. Move. It didn't take long, sometimes just a few minutes outside, but that break helped clear the fog and reset my focus. I'd remind myself: I'm not writing a book just to stay busy. I'm doing this to equip people. To help them break through, just like I had to. You don't need a perfect plan; you need a *pattern interrupt*. The courage to pause, realign, and come back stronger. So when you feel yourself drifting, don't keep pushing through the fog.

Step away.

Reset.

Come back with intention. The best DISC Alignment D-type personality.

Action Steps:

Daily: Interrupt unproductive patterns with a brief reset walk, breathe, journal, or pray.

Weekly: Track when and why your focus drifts so you can prevent it next time.

"I have learned to be content whatever the circumstances... I can do all this through him who gives me strength." Philippians 4:11-13

There was a season when I had a program fully built and ready to launch. The vision was solid. The systems were tight. I had momentum. And then life shifted. My family needed me more deeply in that season. And what I realized was this: The program wasn't the problem. The *pressure* was.

I wasn't building for purpose anymore; I was building from hustle. I was trying to prove something instead of creating something meaningful. So I paused. Not from defeat, but from clarity. I asked myself: *"What does winning look like right now?"* And in that moment, winning looked like peace. It looked like being present. It looked like building something sustainable, not just successful. That pause didn't kill the dream. It refined it.

It gave me the space to build from conviction, not comparison. I'm not here just to execute... I'm here to *become.* Redefining the win gave me back my joy. And now? I build at a pace of grace, not guilt. The best DISC Alignment S-type personality.

Action Steps:

Daily: Revisit your current goals and ask, "Is this driven by purpose or pressure?"

Weekly: Define what success looks like for this season, not forever, just right now.

Story of Transformation:

Genesis' Journey to Elite Volleyball

My daughter Genesis is a great example of what overcoming self-sabotage looks like. Her goal was to become an elite volleyball player, and she had the drive to match it. But like many of us, she faced internal battles. Doubt crept in. She hesitated to try new skills. She second-guessed herself. At times, perfectionism slowed her progress. That's what self-sabotage often looks like—not loud failure, but quiet hesitation that shows up in small moments. But that summer, something shifted.

We talked through the mindset blocks she was facing. We created a plan together and challenged the lies that were holding her back, like needing to be perfect before she could progress. Then we moved into action. Every day, she showed up, trained hard, and gave her best even when it wasn't perfect. She replaced hesitation with intention.

And by the end of the season, Genesis wasn't just a stronger athlete; she was a more confident, focused young woman. Her growth was not just physical, but mental, emotional, and deeply personal.

She learned to stop measuring herself by flawless execution and started defining success as showing up, growing, and pressing forward anyway. Her story is a reminder that a breakthrough begins the moment you stop waiting for perfect... and start fighting for your progress.

Bringing It All Together:

Building Resilience Against Self-Sabotage

Overcoming self-sabotage starts with self-awareness, but it grows through action. You have to identify your triggers, challenge the lies you've believed, interrupt the patterns that keep you stuck, and redefine what success really means *for you.*

This chapter isn't just about recognizing the problem. It's about stepping fully into your purpose with clarity, focus, and courage.

What three self-sabotaging behaviors would you like to overcome?

_____

_____

_____

What three new beliefs can you adopt to counter limiting beliefs?

_____

_____

_____

What three manageable goals can you set to make consistent progress?

_____

_____

_____

Final Reflection:

Choosing to Grow Beyond Self-Sabotage

Self-sabotage may have slowed you down in the past, but it doesn't get the final word. You are not stuck. You are simply standing at a decision point. And now, you have the tools to move forward. Choose progress over perfection. Choose truth over lies. Choose purpose over pressure. Because when you get out of your own way, you unlock the greatness that's been there all along.

CHAPTER 12: EMBRACING THE

UNSTOPPABLE BELIEF MINDSET

The Journey of Unstoppable Belief

As you reach the end of this book, take a moment to reflect on how far you've come. *Unstoppable Belief* was never meant to be just another book; it's a guide, a companion for your journey, and a reminder that no dream is too big, no setback too final, and no goal out of reach.

Every story, strategy, and action step in these pages was designed to equip you with tools to face challenges, stay focused, and grow stronger in the face of resistance.

Growth Isn't Always Easy, But It's Always Worth It

Resilience isn't just about pushing through hard times; it's about learning and growing because of them. Growth doesn't always look or feel good in the moment. It requires letting go of comfort zones, facing old fears, and sometimes rewriting the stories you've believed about yourself. However, if there's one thing I hope you've seen, it's this: you are stronger than you think. Keep showing up. Even on the hard days. Even when it's inconvenient. Even when your belief feels borrowed. Because those are the moments that grow your roots deeper.

Celebrate the Small Wins

Don't wait for the "big moment" to validate your journey. Celebrate the small wins—the early mornings, the tough decisions, the quiet discipline when no one else sees it. Setbacks will happen. But remember, they don't disqualify you, they shape you. Every detour, delay, and disappointment can be a setup for something better if you let it teach you.

Stay Anchored in Purpose

You've heard this again and again in these chapters: your "why" matters. When the road gets tough, reconnect with it. Let your purpose center you. This isn't just about getting things done. It's about becoming who you're meant to be while doing them.

Don't Do It Alone

Unstoppable belief is built in community. You weren't made to walk this journey by yourself. Surround yourself with people who remind you of your greatness, who challenge you when you shrink, and who hold you accountable to the version of you that's rising. When you borrow belief from the right people, you gain the courage to take your next step even when you're not sure where it will lead.

Living with an Unstoppable Belief Mindset

The *Unstoppable Belief* mindset isn't just about pushing harder, it's about staying rooted, getting back up, and believing again. It's choosing faith over fear. Progress over perfection. Purpose over pressure. And here's the truth: you don't need to have it all figured out to begin.

You just need to begin and commit to not giving up when it gets tough.

Final Thoughts

As you close this book, I want to challenge you: don't just finish, follow through. These chapters aren't the end. They're a launchpad. The tools are in your hands now. What you do with them is up to you. You were created for impact. You are equipped for growth. And you have everything inside of you to finish what you started. Let this be your moment to rise, to take action, and to walk boldly in your Unstoppable belief... until it becomes your own.

Chapter 13

UNSTOPPABLE BELIEF FRAMEWORK

FAITH & PERSONALITY INTEGRATION GUIDE

Here Are The Scriptures For Each Chapter Of The Book to include the DISC breakdown and why.

CHAPTER 1: COMPLETE OPTIMIZATION

Scripture: *Now to Him who is able to do immeasurably more than all we ask or imagine, according to His power that is at work within us." Ephesians 3:20 (NIV)*

Step 1: Power Up – Optimize Your Health

Scripture: *"Do you not know that your bodies are temples of the Holy Spirit...? Therefore honor God with your bodies." —1 Corinthians 6:19–20 (NIV)*

Best DISC Alignment: C (Conscientious) **Why:** C-types value structure, personal standards, and self-discipline. This step appeals to their focus on detail and precision in daily habits.

Step 2: Create a Motivational Environment

Scripture: *"Let all things be done decently and in order."*

—1 Corinthians 14:40 (KJV)

Best DISC Alignment: S (Steady) **Why:** S-types thrive in consistent, calm environments. They prefer harmony and order, and this pillar reinforces how their physical space can affect mental peace.

Step 3: Keep Your Gas Tank Full

Scripture: *"Come to me, all you who are weary and burdened, and I will give you rest."* —Matthew 11:28 (NIV)

Best DISC Alignment: I (Influential) **Why:** I-types often burn out from overcommitment and people-pleasing. This reminder to pause, breathe, and rest encourages them to refuel so they can show up joyfully.

Step 4: Make Your Goals Visible

Scripture: *"Where there is no vision, the people perish: but he that keepeth the law, happy is he." Proverbs 29:18*

Best DISC Alignment: D (Dominant) **Why:** D-types are future-focused, driven by results and vision. Visible goals fuel their momentum and help them lead themselves and others with clarity.

Reflection Summary for Chapter 1

- **C** types will resonate most with health systems and self-discipline
- **S** types will appreciate the peace of optimized environments
- **I** types need permission to rest and refuel for sustainability
- **D** types will thrive on bold, visible goals that fuel performance

CHAPTER 2: LEAVING YOUR COMFORT ZONE

Scripture: *"Be strong and courageous. Do not be afraid or terrified because of them, for the Lord your God goes with you..."* —Deuteronomy 31:6 (NIV) *This verse captures the courage and trust required to leave what's familiar and step into growth.*

Step 1: Be a Doer, Not Just a Thinker

Scripture: *"But be doers of the word, and not hearers only, deceiving yourselves."* —James 1:22 (NKJV)

Best DISC Alignment: D – (Dominant) Why: D-types are action-oriented and thrive on decision-making. This step affirms their drive while also calling out the importance of acting from purpose, not pressure.

Step 2: Use FIDO – Forget It and Drive On

Scripture: *"But one thing I do: Forgetting what is behind and straining toward what is ahead..."* —Philippians 3:13 (NIV)

Best DISC Alignment: S – (Steady) **Why:** S-types value harmony and can struggle with conflict or emotional residue. FIDO gives them a framework to process emotion without getting stuck, so they can move forward in peace.

Step 3: Small Wins, Strong Confidence

Scripture: *"Whoever can be trusted with very little can also be trusted with much..."* —Luke 16:10 (NIV)

Best DISC Alignment: C – (Conscientious) **Why:** C-types thrive on clarity, consistency, and structure. Celebrating micro-goals appeals to their strength in breaking down progress into manageable, measurable wins.

Scripture: *"And we know that in all things God works for the good of those who love him..."* —Romans 8:28 (NIV)

Best DISC Alignment: I – (Influential) **Why:** I-types are relationship-focused and can take failure personally. Reframing challenges as opportunities fuels their optimism and helps them re-center on their purpose.

- **D**: Lead with action, not overthinking
- **I**: Reframe failure as feedback, not rejection
- **S**: Practice emotional resilience & graceful release
- **C**: Build confidence through intentional progress

CHAPTER 3: EMBRACING MISTAKES

Scripture: *"Though the righteous fall seven times, they rise again."* —Proverbs 24:16 (NIV) *This sets the tone: mistakes aren't the end they're how we rise.*

Step 1: Take Purposeful Risks to Grow

Scripture: *"Commit to the Lord whatever you do, and He will establish your plans."* —Proverbs 16:3 (NIV)

Best DISC Alignment: D – (Dominant) **Why:** D-types are risk-takers by nature. This step invites them to take bold action while trusting God to guide the outcome, aligning risk with purpose.

Step 2: Practice "Press On" Thinking

Scripture: *"Not that I have already obtained all this... but I press on to take hold of that for which Christ Jesus took hold of me."* —Philippians 3:12 (NIV)

Best DISC Alignment: S – (Steady) **Why:** S-types may struggle with emotional bumps along the journey. "Pressing on" helps them shift gently from shame to growth, offering the steady resilience they value.

Scripture: *"Do not despise these small beginnings, for the Lord rejoices to see the work begin..."* —Zechariah 4:10 (NLT)

Best DISC Alignment: C – (Conscientious) **Why:** C-types often aim for perfection and overlook progress. This principle encourages them to acknowledge growth in both success and missteps, without self-criticism.

Scripture: *"The Lord makes firm the steps of the one who delights in him; though he may stumble, he will not fall, for the Lord upholds him with his hand."* — Psalm 37:23–24 (NIV)

Best DISC Alignment: I – (Influential) **Why:** I-types may take failure personally or avoid reflecting on mistakes. This step teaches them to reframe and redirect with joy and hope.

- **D**: Channel boldness into purposeful risks

- **I**: Reframe failure as growth, not rejection

- **S**: Practice emotional resilience & forward focus

- **C**: Track small progress to build confidence

CHAPTER 4: MASTERING SELF-TALK

Scripture: "For as he thinks in his heart, so is he." This verse speaks directly to the power of our inner dialogue and sets the tone for mastering self-talk and internal belief. Proverbs 23:7 (NKJV)

Step 1: Replace Doubts with Affirmations

Scripture: "So is my word that goes out from my mouth: It will not return to me empty, but will accomplish what I desire..." Isaiah 55:11 (NIV)

Best DISC Alignment: I – (Influential) **Why:** I-types thrive on uplifting language. Affirmations fuel their energy and confidence to rise beyond doubt

Step 2: Identify and Challenge Limiting Beliefs

Scripture: "Let God transform you into a new person by changing the way you think." Romans 12:2 (NLT)

Best DISC Alignment: C – (Conscientious) **Why:** C-types value truth, logic, and deep self-evaluation. Challenging limiting beliefs fits their desire for clarity and accuracy

Step 3: Practice Self-Compassion

Scripture: "As a father has compassion on his children, so the Lord has compassion on those who fear him." Psalm 103:13–14 (NIV)

Best DISC Alignment: S – (Steady) **Why:** S-types often extend compassion to others but need reminders to give it to themselves. This step helps them grow in self-kindness.

Step 4: Mastering Self Through Challenges

Scripture: "I can do all this through him who gives me strength." - Philippians 4:13 (NIV)

Best DISC Alignment: D – (Dominant) **Why:** D-types respond to bold, forward-focused self-talk and visualizing success as a strategy for confidence and action.

Reflection Summary for Chapter 3

- **D**: Transform self-talk into a tool for action
- **I**: Reframe doubts as opportunities for growth
- **S**: Cultivate self-compassion for personal resilience
- **C**: Challenge limiting beliefs with truth and logic

CHAPTER 5: YOUR MOST VALUABLE ASSET

Scripture: "Love your neighbor as yourself." *We can only love and lead others well when we've first learned to value ourselves as God does.* Matthew 22:39 (NIV)

Step 1: Identify Your Strengths and Passions

Scripture: "We have different gifts, according to the grace given to each of us..." *This step helps readers lean into their God-given design.* Romans 12:6 (NIV)

Best DISC Alignment: I – (Influential) **Why:** I-types thrive on creativity and energy. Recognizing their gifts fuels their desire to influence and connect.

Step 2: Set Aside Time for Self-Improvement

Scripture: "Do your best to present yourself to God as one approved, a worker who does not need to be ashamed..." *Intentional growth honors God and builds personal capacity.* 2 Timothy 2:15 (NIV)

Best DISC Alignment: C – (Conscientious) **Why:** C-types love structured learning and development. This step appeals to their desire for excellence and thoroughness.

Step 3: Build a Support System for Growth

Scripture: "Two are better than one... If either of them falls down, one can help the other up." *Growth thrives in community, not isolation.* Ecclesiastes 4:9–10 (NIV)

Best DISC Alignment: S – (Steady) **Why:** S-types value loyalty and relational safety. A trusted support system helps them grow steadily and with confidence.

Step 4: Create a Personal Development Plan

Scripture: "Good planning and hard work lead to prosperity, but hasty shortcuts lead to poverty." *Clarity and consistency create sustainable progress.* Proverbs 21:5 (NLT)

Best DISC Alignment: D – (Dominant) **Why:** D-types are goal-driven. A personal plan gives them a strategic edge and motivation to act decisively.

Reflection Summary for Chapter 5

- **D**: Invest in your future with a growth plan
- **I**: Discover your passion and influence
- **S**: Surround yourself with steady support
- **C**: Prioritize structured self-improvement

Scripture: "Mark out a straight path for your feet; stay on the safe path." Proverbs 4:26 (NLT) *True power begins when we take ownership of our direction and stop giving it away to things we can't control*

Step 1: Identify What You Can Control

Scripture: "Pay careful attention to your own work... For we are each responsible for our own conduct." Galatians 6:4–5 (NLT)

Best DISC Alignment: C – (Conscientious) **Why***:* C-types value structure and focus. This step affirms their strength in narrowing focus to what matters and letting go of the rest.

Step 2: Set Clear Intentions for Your Day

Scripture: "So teach us to number our days that we may get a heart of wisdom." Psalm 90:12 (ESV)

Best DISC Alignment: S – (Steady) **Why**: S-types thrive on routines and purpose. Setting daily intentions helps them feel emotionally safe and motivated.

Step 3: Respond Instead of Reacting

Scripture: "A gentle answer turns away wrath, but a harsh word stirs up anger." Proverbs 15:1 (NIV)

Best DISC Alignment: I – (Influential) **Why**: I-types can be quick to speak and feel. This step empowers them to pause, regulate, and influence with emotional intelligence.

Step 4: Create a Personal Accountability System

Scripture: "Commit your actions to the Lord, and your plans will succeed." — *Proverbs 16:3 (NLT)*

Best DISC Alignment: D – (Dominant) **Why**: D-types are driven by results. An accountability system helps them stay on mission and finish strong.

Reflection Summary for Chapter 6

- **D:** Stay focused and accountable with clear vision

- **I:** Pause before reacting—respond with wisdom

- **S:** Create a daily rhythm rooted in purpose & peace

- **C:** Narrow focus to what's within your control

CHAPTER 7: BUILDING RESILIENCE

Scripture: "Consider it pure joy, my brothers and sisters, whenever you face trials of many kinds, because you know that the testing of your faith produces perseverance. Let perseverance finish its work so that you may be mature and complete, not lacking anything."

— James 1:2–4 (NIV)

Step 1: The Practice of Daily Reflection

Scripture: *"Examine yourselves to see whether you are in the faith; test yourselves." — 2 Corinthians 13:5 (NIV)*

Best DISC Alignment: C (Conscientious) **Why:** C-types love structured routines, introspection, and personal growth. This step empowers them to use quiet evaluation to improve.

Step 2: Celebrate Progress, No Matter How Small

Scripture: "This is the day the Lord has made; we will rejoice and be glad in it." — *Psalm 118:24 (NKJV)*

Best DISC Alignment: I (Influential) **Why:** I-types thrive on joy and positive reinforcement. This step helps them recognize daily victories, boosting their confidence and energy.

Step 3: Extract Lessons from Setbacks

Scripture: "And we know that in all things God works for the good of those who love him, who have been called according to his purpose." — *Romans 8:28 (NIV)*

Best DISC Alignment: D (Dominant) **Why:** D-types are action-oriented but can be hard on themselves. This step reminds them that even setbacks are fuel for growth and future wins.

Scripture: "Let your eyes look straight ahead; fix your gaze directly before you." — *Proverbs 4:25 (NIV)*

Best DISC Alignment: S (Steady) **Why:** S-types are loyal and consistent. Reconnecting with purpose gives them peace, direction, and motivation to keep showing up with heart.

Reflection Summary for Chapter 7

- **D:** Turn setbacks into strategy & forward motion
- **I:** Celebrate small wins to stay inspired
- **S:** Revisit your purpose to stay grounded during challenges
- **C:** Use daily reflection to build lasting inner strength

CHAPTER 8: PRACTICING PATIENCE

Scripture: "Let us not become weary in doing good, for at the proper time we will reap a harvest if we do not give up." This chapter teaches that success is a process. Patience positions us to keep sowing even when results aren't immediate. Galatians 6:9 (NIV)

Step 1: Setting Long-Term and Short-Term Goals

Scripture: "Write the vision and make it plain... Though it tarries, wait for it; because it will surely come, it will not delay." Pairing long-term vision with short-term wins builds momentum and purpose. Habakkuk 2:2–3 (NLT)

Best DISC Alignment: C – (Conscientious) Why: C-types thrive on structure and planning. This step allows them to map out the details and track steady progress.

Step 2: Shift Your Perspective

Scripture: "Do not conform to the pattern of this world, but be transformed by the renewing of your mind." Changing how you see the journey opens doors to joy and alignment. Romans 12:2 (NIV)

Best DISC Alignment: I – (Influential) **Why:** I-types are driven by meaning and impact. When their perspective shifts toward purpose over pressure, their creativity and influence thrive.

Step 3: Honor the Season You're In

Scripture: "There is a time for everything, and a season for every activity under the heavens." Every season— whether fast or slow—is a part of your development.

Ecclesiastes 3:1 (NIV)

Best DISC Alignment: S – (Steady) **Why:** S-types prefer stability and consistency. Learning to trust the current season gives them peace and steady growth.

Step 4: Trust the Timing

Scripture: "But those who hope in the Lord will renew their strength... They will run and not grow weary, they will walk and not be faint." Trusting God's timing brings strength in waiting and power in progress. Isaiah 40:31 (NIV)

Best DISC Alignment: D – (Dominant) **Why:** D-types want results quickly. This step encourages them to pause, trust the process, and lean into long-term impact.

Reflection Summary for Chapter 8

- **D:** Trust the process even when progress feels slow

- **I:** Focus on purpose, not pressure

- **S:** Find peace by honoring your current season

- **C:** Build structure through small goals that fuel the bigger picture

CHAPTER 9: MASTERING FOCUS

Scripture: "Let your eyes look straight ahead; fix your gaze directly before you. Give careful thought to the paths for your feet... do not turn to the right or the left." Staying focused on what matters most brings clarity, progress, and peace. Proverbs 4:25–27 (NIV)

Scripture: "Let us throw off everything that hinders and the sin that so easily entangles. And let us run with perseverance the race marked out for us." Hebrews 12:1 (NIV) Focus begins by letting go of the things that weigh us down.

Best DISC Alignment: D – (Dominant) **Why:** D-types thrive when they have clarity and control. Eliminating distractions helps them stay mission-focused and forward-moving.

Scripture: "There is a time for everything, and a season for every activity under the heavens." Ecclesiastes 3:1 (NIV) Single-tasking honors timing and teaches us to be fully present.

Best DISC Alignment C – (Conscientious) **Why:** C-types value excellence and precision. Focusing on one task at a time allows them to avoid mistakes and deliver their best work.

Step 3: Set Boundaries Around Your Time

Scripture: "Be very careful, then, how you live—not as unwise but as wise, making the most of every opportunity..." Ephesians 5:15–16 (NIV) Time boundaries are a form of wisdom and stewardship.

Best DISC Alignment: S – (Steady) **Why:** S-types are generous and loyal, but can easily become overcommitted. Boundaries protect their energy and honor their values.

Step 4: Prioritize Deep Work

Scripture: "Whatever you do, work at it with all your heart, as working for the Lord, not for human masters." Colossians 3:23 (NIV) Deep work multiplies impact by bringing your full heart and attention to what matters.

Best DISC Alignment I – (Influential) **Why:** I-types are often idea-rich and people-focused. Deep work helps them ground their energy into meaningful progress and purpose.

- **D**: Remove distractions and stay laser-focused on what moves you forward
- **I**: Anchor your energy in deep, purposeful work
- **S**: Create time boundaries to protect what matters
- **C**: Practice single-tasking to sharpen excellence and avoid overwhelm

CHAPTER 10: CREATE ACCOUNTABILITY

Scripture: *"As iron sharpens iron, so one person sharpens another."* Proverbs 27:17 (NIV). True accountability strengthens character, purpose, and perseverance through mutual support.

Step 1: Find an Accountability Partner

Scripture: *"Two are better than one... If either of them falls down, one can help the other up."* Ecclesiastes 4:9–10 (NIV). We grow stronger when we walk alongside others who care enough to correct and encourage.

Best DISC Alignment: S – (Steady) **Why:** S-types value supportive relationships. This step offers the consistent encouragement and trust they naturally desire in growth partnerships.

Step 2: Set Public Commitments

Scripture: *"Let your light shine before others, that they may see your good deeds and glorify your Father in heaven."* Matthew 5:16 (NIV) Public accountability invites both courage and consistency; it pushes your commitment beyond private intention.

Best DISC Alignment: D – (Dominant) **Why:** D-types are action-oriented and motivated by visible results.

Public commitments provide the external drive and clarity they crave to stay focused.

Step 3: Regular Self-Check-Ins

Scripture: *"Let us examine our ways and test them, and let us return to the Lord."* Lamentations 3:40 (NIV) Reflection leads to realignment. Daily self-examination helps you grow in self-awareness and purpose.

Best DISC Alignment: C – (Conscientious) **Why:** C-types excel at analysis and improvement. This step appeals to their desire for structured, intentional progress through reflection and adjustment.

Step 4: Celebrate Milestones with Accountability Partners

Scripture: *"Rejoice with those who rejoice; mourn with those who mourn."* Romans 12:15 (NIV) Celebrating wins together builds trust, joy, and momentum—it affirms that progress is a shared journey.

Best DISC Alignment: I – (Influential) **Why:** I-types thrive in recognition and relational joy. Celebrating with others motivates and uplifts them, creating lasting memories tied to their growth.

Reflection Summary for Chapter 10

- **D:** Use public goals to fuel action
- **I:** Celebrate shared success often
- **S:** Lean into loyal accountability partners
- **C:** Use daily reflection to align and grow

CHAPTER 11: OVERCOMING SELF-SABOTAGE

Scripture: "We take captive every thought to make it obedient to Christ." 2 Corinthians 10:5 (NIV).

Overcoming self-sabotage begins by renewing our minds and challenging the thoughts that keep us stuck.

Step 1: Identify Your Triggers

Scripture: "Search me, God, and know my heart... See if there is any offensive way in me, and lead me in the way everlasting." Psalm 139:23–24 (NIV). Self-awareness is the first step to change. We invite God into the process of uncovering what's holding us back.

Best DISC Alignment: C – (Conscientious) **Why:** C-types are naturally reflective and analytical. They excel at noticing patterns, but may overanalyze. This step empowers them to focus their reflection on healing.

Step 2: Challenge Limiting Beliefs

Scripture: *"Finally, brothers and sisters, whatever is true, whatever is noble, whatever is right... think about such things." — Philippians 4:8 (NIV)* Changing your inner dialogue leads to transformed behavior and belief.

Best DISC Alignment: I – (Influential) **Why:** I-types often wrestle with insecurity masked by charisma. This step equips them to shift inner narratives and use their voice powerfully and truthfully.

Step 3: Interrupt the Pattern

Scripture: "See, I am doing a new thing! Now it springs up; do you not perceive it?" Isaiah 43:19 (NIV) Sometimes a pattern interrupt is what opens us to God's new thing.

Best DISC Alignment: D – (Dominant) **Why:** D-types thrive in action. Interrupting unhelpful behavior and creating new motion fuels their forward momentum and breaks cycles quickly.

Step 4: Redefine the Win

Scripture: "I have learned to be content whatever the circumstances... I can do all this through him who gives me strength." Philippians 4:11–13 (NIV). Redefining success according to God's peace—not pressure—creates freedom and long-term growth.

Best DISC Alignment: S – (Steady) **Why:** S-types value peace, stability, and purpose. Redefining "the win" releases them from people-pleasing and helps them

grow with grace.

- **D:** Interrupt the cycle with intentional action

- **I:** Speak truth over your inner critic

- **S:** Redefine success through peace, not pressure

- **C:** Identify internal triggers with clarity

About the Author

Cristian Martinez is a living testament to resilience, purpose, and transformational leadership. Born and raised on the island of St. Croix in the U.S. Virgin Islands, His foundation was built on faith, humility, and the belief that hard work honors God.

After high school, he embarked on a 23-year career in the United States Air Force, where he rose through the ranks as a respected leader known for his excellence and integrity. Cris served as both the Air Force Global Strike Command and Air Combat Command Optometry Consultant & Functional Manager, providing leadership and operational guidance to 19 locations worldwide. His influence helped ensure the health and readiness of warfighters across the globe.

His leadership legacy includes multiple team and individual honors, such as:

- USAF Medical Treatment Facility of the Year

- Aerospace Medicine Unit of the Year (three times)

- Inspector General Team of the Year

- USAF Surgeon General Hospital of the Year

- Honor Guard Team of the Year

- Lance P. Sijan Leadership Award

- Air Force Ophthalmic NCO of the Year (twice)

- Meager Wiley Evers Outstanding Community Service & Volunteer Awards

- Japan American AirForce Goodwill Association Award

Beyond the uniform, Cris found his deeper calling: developing leaders, building families, and empowering future generations. As the 2022 Maxwell Leadership Xceeding Expectations Award winner, he has trained and mentored thousands across 11 countries, delivering keynote messages, coaching sessions, and transformational leadership programs that ignite personal growth and purpose.

He has also served as President of two Professional Development Non-Profit Organizations, leading memberships of over 2,000 to award-winning impact in leadership, community outreach, and mentorship. Today, Cristian leads Leadership Legacy, a company he co-founded with his wife, Sharita, where together they equip leaders and entrepreneurs, enrich families, and empower youth to rise above limitations and embrace their God-given calling. Whether on stage, in strategy rooms, or one-on-one with emerging leaders, His mission remains the same: To serve, inspire, and lead others into lasting transformation.

Connect with Cristian

Mission: Changing Mindsets One Person at a Time

www.cristianrmartinez.com/culture

Free Training – How to Unlock Your Power: 3 Exercises

to Change Your Life

https://adilo.bigcommand.com/watch/0wjA8_le

Made in the USA
Middletown, DE
04 December 2025

24006723R00126